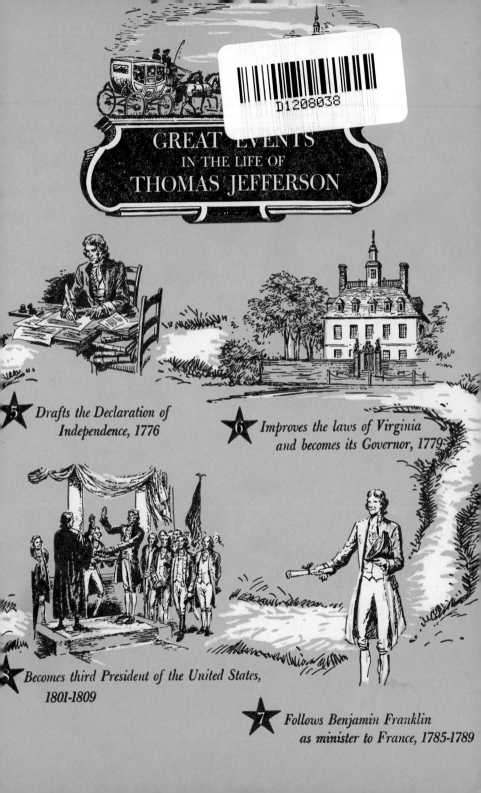

GREAT EVENTS
IN THE LIFE OF
THOMAS JEFFERSON

5 Drafts the Declaration of
Independence, 1776

6 Improves the laws of Virginia
and becomes its Governor, 1779

Becomes third President of the United States,
1801-1809

7 Follows Benjamin Franklin
as minister to France, 1785-1789

THE STORY OF
Thomas Jefferson

Tom stared at the Indian chief

THE STORY OF
Thomas Jefferson

By EARL SCHENCK MIERS

Illustrated by REYNOLD C. POLLAK

PUBLISHERS Grosset & Dunlap NEW YORK

PRINTED IN THE UNITED STATES OF AMERICA
Library of Congress Catalog Card No. 55-10740

For
Billy Miers

Contents

Illustrations

ILLUSTRATIONS

THE STORY OF
Thomas Jefferson

*"Thomas, it is playing the peacock
to scrawl your name on the wall"*

CHAPTER ONE

The Newcomer

THE morning was gray and misty, without a trace of sun, when Tom awoke. The boy rolled over and listened hopefully. Not even a mouse scurrying along a baseboard broke the silence of the house.

"You'd think Jonas would be up by now," Tom grumbled. "It's cold these April mornings. Those downstairs fires should be lighted early."

Then Tom's eight-year-old appetite began to complain. Why wasn't Sary busy in the kitchen, raking up the coals and getting the griddle cakes and hominy ready for breakfast?

Outside a rooster crowed lustily. The boy chuckled.

[*3*]

"If *he's* up, I can get up," Tom muttered. With a leap he reached the washstand.

The morning chilliness made Tom's teeth chatter. He washed like a kitten, believing that he required no more than a lick and a swipe of a paw to be clean. He dressed hurriedly, then squinted into a mirror and ran long fingers through his red, unruly hair.

Creeping softly down the stairs, Tom admitted the real reason he was awake. Had Belinda had her litter during the night? Was the puppy that his father had said he might choose for himself already waiting in the stables?

When Tom opened the front door his courage almost failed him. Everywhere mist hung in ghostly patches above the ground. The cedar trees that grew by the stables looked unreal in the haze and seemed closer together than the boy had remembered. Far below, the swirling, muddy waters of the James River gurgled with a sad, lonesome moan.

Tom shivered. Whenever he heard stories of giants and demons, he was sure that they must hide in misty places like this! Then Tom squared his shoulders. Giants and demons

The morning chilliness made Tom's teeth chatter

weren't going to keep him from seeing his puppy!

Tom fled across the lawn. When he reached the cedars, he stopped, panting, and looked back. How silly he had been to feel scared! There stood Tuckahoe, his home, just as it always had. It was the same H-shaped building, with the same three chimneys and the same twelve steps going up to the front porch!

Tom stepped through the trees and approached the stables. Then his heart jumped. Standing by the stable door was a tall, shadowy figure.

"Good morning, Tom," sang out a familiar voice.

The boy whistled a long sigh of relief. Excitedly he asked, "Father, did Belinda have her puppies?"

Peter Jefferson shook his head. "Sometime before the day is over they'll be here, Tom, but Belinda isn't saying when."

"Can I see her, Father?"

"I wouldn't go in," Mr. Jefferson said. "She's in a cross, snappish mood and tried to bite my hand when I went to pet her a little while ago."

[6]

Tom felt bitterly disappointed, but his father placed an arm around his shoulder. Tom grinned. In all the world, he wouldn't find a better friend than his father. He didn't ask why Tom was up at this silly hour. He understood a boy.

"Is Belinda really an English-bred foxhound?" Tom asked as they walked back through the mists.

"She surely is," Peter Jefferson answered. "I went all the way to Northern Neck to get her from Lord Fairfax after I heard he had imported twenty hounds from England."

"Then my pup will grow into one of the best foxers in Virginia," Tom exclaimed.

"If you train him right."

"I will, I will!" Tom promised. But what he didn't know was how he would live through the day waiting for Belinda to give him his dog to train!

Tom's difficulties began at breakfast.

"Boy," old Sary said crossly, "I didn't cook those grits and griddle cakes to grow cold on your plate."

"I'm not hungry, Miss Sary," Tom said. "I thought I was, but now I can't eat."

[7]

"You can't eat if you don't open your mouth,"
Sary grumbled

"You can't eat if you don't open your mouth and put the food in," Sary grumbled. "You just try that for a change!"

Tom forced down the food. He wanted a dog with good spots. Maybe he would name it Spot.

There were still no puppies when it came time to go to school. Tom groaned. Worst of all, the schoolhouse on Tuckahoe plantation was situated near the stables.

"Somehow you'll live through the morning," Jane Jefferson said understandingly. This pretty, dark-haired sister, who was three years older than Tom, always took his part.

And Mary Jefferson, who was a year younger than Jane, always teased. "Tom's sick with puppy love! Tom's sick with puppy love!"

The younger Jefferson children, Elizabeth and Martha, took up the chant. The Randolph cousins joined in. Tom looked stormily away. No one had promised *them* one of Belinda's puppies. They were green-eyed with jealousy!

"Leave Tom alone or I'll whip the lot of you," Jane threatened furiously.

The others fell silent, but Tom suspected that they were snickering behind his back. Grimly, he went into the schoolroom and took his seat. He stared at the plaster wall and realized with a stab of guilt that he had not washed off his name where he had scrawled it yesterday afternoon! Likely he would catch it good for that this morning! Troubles always came in pairs, his mother said.

Tom tried to follow his lessons. How long the first hour of reading seemed! But the next hour of arithmetic went even more slowly. Tom gritted his teeth. He just wouldn't think of Belinda and the stables. Still his mind wandered.

Tuckahoe wasn't really his home, Tom thought. Yet he couldn't recall anything about Shadwell, the house in the mountains near Charlottesville, Virginia, where he had been born. He had been only two when the Jeffersons had moved to the Randolph plantation, their present home, two miles below the Richmond Falls.

"Why don't we go back to Shadwell?" Tom often asked his father. Always the answer was the same:

"Tom, the man who lived here was my dearest friend. I promised him before he died that I would care for Tuckahoe until his children could do so by themselves. A man of honor lives by his word."

Lost in these daydreams, Tom did not hear the schoolmaster calling his name. Again, sternly, the teacher said, "Thomas!"

"Yes, sir," Tom answered, jumping up as though he had been stuck with a pin. He blushed at the giggles behind him.

"Thomas, did you study the rules of good behavior in the book I gave you?"

"Yes, sir!"

The schoolmaster stroked his chin. "Give the first rule of good conduct when in the presence of others," the teacher demanded.

"Sing not to yourself with a humming noise, nor drum with your fingers or feet," Tom recited.

"And what," the schoolmaster insisted, "is the rule about your clothes?"

Tom answered: "Wear not your clothes foul or dusty, but see that they are brushed once every day at least."

"Now the rule against vanity."

"This is the one," he told his father

Tom drew a deep breath. But the giggles had stopped. Even half asleep, his memory never failed him. Once more Tom knew the rule: "Play not the peacock, looking everywhere about you to see if your shoes fit well or your stockings sit neatly or your clothes hang handsomely."

The schoolmaster nodded. "Thomas, it is playing the peacock to scrawl your name on the wall. See that it is washed off!"

Tom gulped. "Yes, sir!" he said meekly.

But there was a twinkle in the schoolmaster's eyes. "I see your father coming from the stables," he remarked. "Could he be looking for you?"

Tom's heart leaped. Belinda must have had her litter! The schoolmaster nodded, excusing Tom for a few minutes.

At the sight of Tom's flushed, eager face, Peter Jefferson broke into a laugh.

"There are four pups, Tom," he said. "Every one is a beauty. You'll find it a hard choice to make."

Inside the stables, Belinda seemed proud of her young ones. She was now quite docile and let Tom scratch the inside of her long ears.

[*13*]

Three of the pups nestled against their mother. Tom found the fourth trying to stand on his wobbly legs.

"You were born a snoopy rascal," Tom chuckled.

He picked up the pup. Its coat was white with black and tan patches. Carefully the boy felt its legs, its underbelly, its curving throat.

Tom pressed the dog's nose to his cheek. He sighed happily.

"This is the one," he told his father.

"What will you call him, Tom?"

The boy laughed. "Snoop," he said.

[*14*]

CHAPTER TWO

Night Fires

THE following summer, when Tom was
nine, Mr. Jefferson announced one day, "The
Randolphs can run Tuckahoe now. Next
week we can return to our own home."

Mrs. Jefferson looked very happy. "Seven
years have been a long time to be away from
Shadwell," she said. "I shall like managing
my own house again."

For the next few days Tuckahoe hummed
with the packing that went with moving. A
day early, the family servants drove off in wag-
ons loaded with furniture, trunks, and a cask
filled with live carp from the James River that
Mr. Jefferson was taking to stock his streams
at Shadwell.

Packing was no great problem to Tom. All he needed to do was to whistle for Snoop and he was ready to go.

The Jeffersons, mounted on their horses, left after breakfast. When the afternoon shadows lengthened, they were still traveling.

Mrs. Jefferson laughed at Tom's dog. Snoop bounced down the road on agile legs. When he disappeared in the tall grass, rabbits scurried in all directions and birds winged skyward.

"Tom, you gave that hound the right name," Mrs. Jefferson declared. "He snoops into everything!"

Tom nodded. Never once, during the long journey from Tuckahoe to Shadwell, had Snoop rested. Now, deep in the Virginia highlands, the wild, unbroken hills were filled with scents to tickle the nose of a foxhound.

Little Martha looked uneasy. "How thick the forest is," she complained. "Why, this is the edge of the wilderness!"

But Jane cried, "There won't be any old James River mosquitoes here to bite and bite."

And Elizabeth Jefferson added, "Or any old bullfrogs stuck in the mud all night keeping you awake with their croaking."

Mrs. Jefferson spoke firmly. "Wherever the family is together, we'll be happy."

Jane Jefferson rode up to talk to Tom. "Why the frown?" she asked.

"I just remembered something," he confessed. "I never did wash my name off that schoolroom wall!"

"Well, none of your lazy cousins will do it for you," Jane said. "You'll just have to become a famous man, Tom, so that the Randolphs can point with pride to that scrawl."

The boy grinned. "There's slim chance of that," he predicted.

Peter Jefferson gave a sudden shout. "Around the next turn you'll see Shadwell!"

Tom couldn't wait. He was like Snoop, filled with the excitement of new things. He spurred his horse ahead.

The boy saw first the tall, broad chimneys that stood like sentinels at either end of the sprawling, two-story house. He liked the veranda in front, for here was the place to romp on rainy days. Fine old trees, right for swings and climbing, filled the yard. Far overhead a graceful hawk dipped its wings.

"We're going to have fun at Shadwell," Tom announced to Snoop.

The foxhound wagged his tail.

For Tom, discovering the mysteries of his new home filled the next few weeks. He rode everywhere with Snoop prancing beside him. Martha had been right—the highlands around Charlottesville were wild country indeed.

Tom's first mystery was Willis Mountain.

[*19*]

When he looked across rolling fields of tobacco and corn he could see this solitary mountain rising from level ground.

"It has different shapes for different days," he told Jane.

"But it can't," the girl insisted.

"Yes, it does," Tom declared. "Some days it stands up straight and some days it leans. Some days it is round on top and some days it is flat."

"Tom, what will you try to tell me next?" Jane exclaimed. But when she went back to look, she found that her brother was right. Willis Mountain did seem to change shape! "He sees everything," she thought. That mountain was forty miles away.

Almost fifty slaves helped Peter Jefferson cultivate the nineteen hundred acres of his plantation at Shadwell. Within two weeks Tom knew them all by name, and wherever his long legs and carroty top appeared there were smiles of welcome.

"Roasting corn this morning," someone always called when Tom rode by the slave quarters. "You hungry enough to nibble an ear?"

"I sure am," Tom answered, sliding down from his horse.

"Now let me see," the first voice muttered. "Can't leave that Snoop out. Must be a bone around here somewhere for him!"

The houses of the slave quarters stood in a long row, each connected to the next. Inside, the rooms were as clean as the main hall at Shadwell. There was a wide stretch of lawn before the houses, and in late morning the sun made it a drowsy, jolly place.

Snoop also liked the Quarters. Every family seemed to own at least one dog. Snoop raced and rolled and nipped and barked with all of them.

It was through Willie, the stableboy, that Tom first learned the plantation had its own river. Once this lazy, muddy stream had been called the River Anna, but now everybody said Rivanna, running the two words together.

"Old river don't flow fast enough to deserve two names," Willie said with a grin.

"Any bass or pickerel?" Tom asked.

"If you know where to throw your line," Willie replied. "Now, down here a pace there's a funny kind of mound—"

"What sort of mound?" Tom asked when Willie broke off.

"Indian mound, I reckon," Willie mumbled without much enthusiasm.

"Show it to me, Willie!"

Though the other boy was a year older than Tom, he stood almost a foot shorter. Willie raised himself on tiptoe so that he could whisper in Tom's ear.

"That mound's just an old ghost pile," he said. "I don't like that place!"

Excitement glowed in Tom's face. "You mean there are Indians buried there?"

"That's what I mean," Willie said. "That's why there are always fish around there. The haunts make them come there!"

Tom laughed. "You know that isn't so," he exclaimed. "How did the mound get there?"

Willie rolled his eyes uncomfortably. "My daddy says the Indians once had a fight there. Then they just covered up everybody who got killed and went away. Mr. Tom, that's all I know and all I want to know!"

But Tom's curiosity was far from satisfied. "Take me there, Willie," he urged.

Poor Willie looked sick. Never did any pair of feet drag more slowly along the bank of the Rivanna than did the feet of Willie. Presently he stopped and wiped a hand across his face.

[23]

"There's your old ghost pile," he said.

Snoop bounded joyously ahead and Tom followed.

The ground was low where the mound stood, though across the stream rose pleasant hills. Tom doubted Willie's story about the battle. In olden times an Indian town could have stood on the hill and this could have been its burial ground.

Tom judged that the mound must be about forty feet across at its base. Around it was a ditch some five feet deep from which the dirt for the mound had been dug.

A leap carried Tom across the ditch and up the slope of the hillock. Trees and scrub covered the slopes and at the summit Tom stood seven or eight feet above Willie's head. The soil showed marks of plow cuts. Once the mound must have been much higher than it now stood.

Tom's excitement grew. He returned to the place where Willie stood twisting one leg against the other.

"Will you help me dig in that mound to see what's there?" Tom pleaded.

"I got work to do in the stables," Willie objected.

"But I'll ask Father to let you help me," Tom said.

Willie sucked in his breath, determined to make Tom see the truth. "Being around horses I like," he grumbled. "Being around ghosts I don't like."

All right, Tom thought. Then he would dig by himself. That night he couldn't fall asleep, wondering what he would find in the mound.

Tom looked through the window to see if the stars were out. His eyes turned toward the spot where the mound was situated. Suddenly a chill raced down his spine.

Tom could swear that he saw a circle of campfires not far from the mound. He stared down into the valley. Distinctly he saw a flame leap into the air as though someone had stirred up a fire. He listened intently.

Yes, Tom told himself, on the freshening breeze that blew from across the Rivanna he could hear faint sounds of voices.

The boy gulped. Did Willie's ghosts come out of their mound at night and sing and dance in the moonlight as ghosts did in legends?

"But this is real," Tom said in a hushed voice. "This is no storybook!"

Another chill raced along Tom's back. Down by the stables Snoop began to bark.

CHAPTER THREE

The Big Buffalo

As THAT second shiver ran down the boy's spine, a voice floated across the room.

"Tom!" it called softly. "Are you awake, Tom?"

Tom almost bolted out of bed.

"It's Father," Peter Jefferson whispered from the doorway. "Bring your clothes and come quietly so as not to awaken the other children."

In the hallway Tom asked breathlessly, "Did you see the campfires?"

The man nodded.

"What does it mean, Father?"

"A group of Indians are spending the night down there," Peter Jefferson answered.

[27]

"You—mean—*live* Indians?" Tom blurted.

"Very much alive," his father said with a smile. "Every few months a party comes out of the western hills on their way to Williamsburg to see the Governor about their hunting and trading rights. I told Mother I wanted you to meet them, but you've got to promise to stay in bed and make up your lost sleep tomorrow morning."

"Oh, I will," Tom replied eagerly. He seemed to fly into his clothes.

At the stables, while they were saddling the horses, Tom asked, "Can we take Snoop?"

Peter Jefferson chuckled. "I guess we better unless we want that hound to set up a howl that will wake the entire household!"

But now Tom had another question. "Father, will I be able to understand the Indians? Will they talk in sign language?"

"With you," the man said, "they will talk in English. Often the Indian is highly intelligent and learns our ways faster than we learn his."

Snoop wagged his tail and Tom grinned. "Anyhow, I know Snoop's sign language!"

Peter Jefferson laughed.

Tom never had ridden through the highlands at night. He kept his horse close to his father's mount.

"Snoop, you stay where I can hear you," he ordered sternly.

Far off, among the trees, an old owl hooted. Then, closer by, rose a sharp, piercing screech. Tom pulled tight on the rein.

"Wildcat," his father said, a bit stiffly. "A mean beast, but Snoop will give us warning if it comes any nearer."

Tom swallowed and was glad he had noticed his father carrying a gun when they left.

The ride to the Indian encampment was farther than he had expected.

[29]

Sometimes the trees were so thick and tall that he couldn't see the stars. Always, when it was darkest, that old owl started hooting.

Sometimes Snoop bared his teeth in a snarl and pranced uneasily. "You stay here, Snoop," Tom called sharply in such moments, and the dog quieted.

"You've trained that hound well," Peter Jefferson said. Tom felt proud.

Then the road dipped into a hollow and they could see the fires clearly. About a dozen men were grouped around the blazing timbers. Above one of the fires was a spit on which a deer was roasting. Tom's heart began to beat faster.

"I thought so," Peter Jefferson told his son. "These are Cherokees. That fellow who looks about seven feet tall is Ontasseté, their leader. We have met before and are old friends. He speaks very good English."

Tom's father might himself have been a Cherokee for the warm welcome he received on dismounting at the encampment. Ontasseté cried out joyously.

Tom stared at the Indian chief. He *was* the

tallest man the boy had ever seen. He could be every inch of seven feet!

In the firelight, the Cherokee's face seemed grave and seamed, and his dark eyes flashed. His jacket was made of doeskin with bead-work decorating the neck and sleeves. His trousers looked English-made, and doubtless had been bought at a trading post or were a gift from the Governor. His feet were mocca-sined.

As Peter Jefferson's son, Tom also was warmly welcomed.

His father, Tom saw, soon was sitting cross-legged on the ground beside Ontasseté. But Snoop, whose nose twitched at the smell of the roasting meat, gave the boy a problem.

"He want venison like everybody else," laughed the Cherokee who watched the deer.

Tom stood beside this fellow, who seemed almost as big a giant as Ontasseté. In the glow of the fire his coppery skin looked almost the color of Tom's reddish hair.

"Good dog," the Cherokee said. "Legs have lots of bounce. He catch gray fox before fox kills chickens."

"I haven't hunted with him yet," Tom said.

"Good dog," the Indian repeated. As he talked he kept the deer turning on the spit. The fire sputtered with the dripping juices.

How easy it was to get along with the Cherokees, Tom thought. All were friendly and talkative. One mended a moccasin while he awaited his supper. Another carved a stick and Tom saw that at one end he had shaped the head of a bear.

"Make doll for little papoose at home," the woodcarver told Tom.

After a time Ontasseté went to look at the deer. "You both must eat with us," he said to Peter Jefferson.

Tom held in both hands the slice of venison that was carved for him with Ontasseté's own hunting knife. The juices dripped down his chin.

"Not always did the Cherokee eat this well," Ontasseté said. "That is quite a story."

"Tell it to us," Peter Jefferson urged.

The Indians shouted for the story. Once Ontasseté began the tale, Tom understood why. The Cherokee's voice was filled with a deep, thrilling melody that blended with the crackling of the campfires. He talked as one who knew all the tales and legends of the Cherokees and spoke of them so that they would never be forgotten.

"It all happened long ago," Ontasseté began.

"How long?" Tom asked.

"No one can remember," Ontasseté said.

"That is so," another Cherokee chanted.

"And the people were hungry," Ontasseté said. "For the Big Buffalo were here and they were demons."

"How big were they?" Tom insisted.

"My son, they were as big as young trees," Ontasseté answered. "Their heads were as big as my outstretched arms, and a horse could stand on their shoulders. The people starved, Everything went to feed these monsters."

"They ate all the deer and elk and bear," one Cherokee sang.

"All the corn," another cried.

"Everything that was created for the use of the Indian went down their throats," a third intoned.

[*33*]

"Then how could anybody live?" Tom exclaimed.

Ontasseté's eyes snapped. He wrenched off a bite of meat. "My son," he said, chewing slowly, "the Great Man above saw. He was enraged. He seized his lightning and descended to earth. This was in the valley of the great river called the Ohio. He seated himself on a neighboring mountain and planted his feet on the rocks."

"The prints are still there," another cried.

"By the Big Salt Licks," a comrade declared.

Ontasseté nodded solemnly. "It is all true," he continued. "And sitting there on the mountain, the Great Man hurled his bolts of lightning among the Big Buffalo until the whole herd were slaughtered—all but the big bull."

"But how did he escape?" Tom asked.

"The bull turned his forehead to the shafts of lightning," Ontasseté continued, "and shook them off as they fell. But at length he missed one. The bull was terribly wounded in the side. He turned with a spring, and bounded over the Ohio."

[34]

"And over the Wabash," sang a tall Cherokee.

"And over the Illinois," added the Indian who tended the roasted deer.

"And finally," Ontasseté concluded, "he bounded over the Great Lakes, where he is living to this day."

For a time, after Ontasseté finished, the only sound Tom heard was the wood snapping and splitting on the fires. Then the Cherokees broke into a shout for more venison. Their spirit grew jovial, and Tom guessed that Ontasseté's story of the Big Buffalo had a deep meaning for them. The Great Man above was their protector. Every bit of food they ever ate he gave to them.

Suddenly the Cherokees burst into a chant. Hands were clapped in unison as the music increased in volume. And one old fellow, with fringe hanging from the bottom of his buckskin jacket and big rings fastened in his ears, jumped to his feet and began to prance around the fires.

Tom's hand held Snoop, who strained to chase after the dancer.

"They are expressing their thanks for the

[35]

food they have eaten," Peter Jefferson whispered to Tom.

The boy watched in fascination, for the old fellow's nimble legs stepped higher and higher. The dance ended with another shout.

Tom's father stood up. It was time to leave. Ontasseté came over and placed his hand on Tom's shoulder.

"My son," the Cherokee said, "you will always be our friend. We shall look forward to seeing you again."

"I am glad to be your friend," Tom answered.

"Someday," Ontasseté went on, "you must visit us."

Tom nodded eagerly. Already his imagination had been stirred by the names of the rivers he had heard in the story of the Big Buffalo —the Ohio and Wabash and Illinois. What a wonderful country there must be to explore beyond the mountains of Virginia!

On the ride back to Shadwell, Tom again rode his horse beside his father's.

"I wish I could tell a story like Ontassetè," Tom burst out. "His voice is like music."

In the darkness Peter Jefferson smiled. "None of us can do everything well," he said. "It doesn't matter."

Once more in the distance the old owl hooted. But the wildcat prowled elsewhere, and the forest otherwise was silent.

"The Cherokees are fine people," Tom said.

Again the darkness hid his father's smile. "Tom," the man said, *"people* are fine, whether they be English or Indian."

"Or are born into slavery," Tom added.

"Yes," Peter Jefferson answered. "I am glad you believe that, Tom."

The ride was over all too soon for Tom. There wasn't any experience in his whole life better than being able to talk with his father as man to man!

CHAPTER FOUR

Tom Does His Share

AFTER the visit of Ontasseté and the Cherokees, Tom was more eager than ever to explore the Indian mound. But now Peter Jefferson as well as Willie frowned on that idea.

"Tom," his father said, "there is a time for play and a time for work. It is late August and the tobacco must be harvested and cured. Your digging can wait where the crop won't."

The boy tried to hide his disappointment, but a telltale scowl darkened his eyes.

"Some day Shadwell will belong to you," Peter Jefferson continued. "You must learn all you can about running a plantation, for many people will depend on you for their living. You are a planter, Tom—a farmer's son. I want you to be a good one."

Tom knew that his father was right. Only by doing his share of the work could he really learn how to be a successful planter. The scowl disappeared, and in another moment he was grinning.

"It wouldn't be much fun, anyhow, being left out of what everybody else was doing," he decided.

"We'll have work for anyone able to help," Peter Jefferson agreed.

During the next few days cutting and curing the tobacco was all anyone thought or talked about. Down in the slave quarters women prodded the men in stern voices:

"Now you all hustle out in those fields where you're needed. We can feed the pigs and chickens and milk the cows and tend the horses. Don't you come back here till Massa Peter tells you. Come eating time, we'll bring the meals out to you!"

At the main house meals waited until the work in the fields allowed Tom and his father to come up for them.

"Look there," cried Willie, cutting in the same row with Tom. "We sure grew good tobacco this year."

Tom nodded. The plants had grown to heights of six and seven feet. The leaves, coming out of the tough, thick stalk, sometimes fanned across the row to a length of three feet,

and a leaf, when opened, might measure sixteen inches across.

Willie had a strong pair of arms, and chopped off the leaves with a quick, clean

stroke of his long knife. Tom followed behind, tying the leaves together so that they
could be hung over sticks and carried to the
log-hewn sheds for curing.

The process of curing the tobacco was the
one to which Peter Jefferson gave greatest
attention. In each of the lean-tos, where the
tobacco was hung, fires were lighted and
watched constantly.

"You don't want the temperature of your
shed to change," Tom's father told him. "In
anywhere from thirty to forty hours you'll see
those green leaves turn to lemon-yellow."

Tom went from fire to fire, making sure
that each burned steadily and that the smoke
did not reach the tobacco. At a shift in wind
he would set up a yell for any boy who was
near:

"Willie! Nat! You, Caesar! Come a-running
and help me fan."

And fan with a grim will they all did, driving away the smoke that could have ruined
their leaves.

Meanwhile, beside the sheds, hammers
pounded noisily as other workers, who were

[*41*]

called coopers, built the large hogsheads into which the dried tobacco must be packed for shipment.

"I always like to see the first hogshead go off," Peter Jefferson said cheerfully. "You feel then as though your work has meant something."

Tom shared his father's pride in the fine tobacco Shadwell had produced that year. On a plantation people knew how to take care of themselves. Weeks ago when the tops had been cut off the tobacco plants so that all of the growth would go into the leaves, this was the time of which all had been thinking.

But even hard work wasn't enough to bring a good crop like this. It had been a lucky year —not too much sun or too much rain. Tom, thinking of how fortunate they had been, forgot that the soil at Shadwell was stained with a reddish substance. Now, when he wiped his face, he left streaks there that wouldn't wash off in a week.

Peter Jefferson laughed at his son.

"You look like a painted Indian on the warpath," he declared. "It will wear off in time.

And a little dirt never hurt any farmer!"

The great day arrived. Tobacco that had dried and changed in color to a lemon-yellow was packed into the first hogshead. Tom helped to lift up the leaves. The lid was pounded on with eager blows of a hammer, and heavy leather thongs were wound around the sides.

The hogshead then was hitched to a frame drawn by an ox, and a horse was chained in front to lead the ox. Willie's father was to drive the first team and Willie perched proudly on the horse.

[43]

"Giddap, there!" the man shouted. His whip snapped.

Everyone around the sheds stopped working to watch. The animals, heads lowered, strained forward. Slowly, the hogshead began to roll.

"There she goes," someone cheered.

"Keep her a-rolling to the river," another shouted.

But a third voice spoke sternly. "Get back to your work, you idlers! Pack that next hogshead. We've got a lot of rolling to do before you all can dance for your suppers!"

With good-natured shouts, the men returned to packing. On tiptoe, Tom watched Willie bobbing on the back of the horse. His figure grew smaller as the team lumbered down the hill toward the Rivanna. Here, loaded on barges, the tobacco would begin its long journey to the market in Richmond.

All through that day and the next the scene was repeated. Sometimes there would be three or four hogsheads rolling down to the Rivanna at the same time and as many teams coming back for new loads.

"We're going to have us a wing-ding down to the Quarters tonight," Willie announced when at last the final hogshead was packed. "Always a good reason for kicking up your heels when the crop's on its way to market."

"Can we go?" Tom begged his father.

"We certainly can," Peter Jefferson said. "The girls and Mother, too. And, Tom, maybe you better bring your fiddle!"

What Willie called "a wing-ding" seemed at first to be a contest to see who could eat the most. Peter Jefferson had ordered three pigs slaughtered and roasted. A dozen chickens had gone to the same fate. And under the coals of every fire corn in the husk and potatoes roasted.

Tom ate till he groaned. Peter Jefferson chuckled. "It's a poor farmer who doesn't celebrate his harvest," he said.

A shout went up. Hands began clapping. Deep voices broke into song.

"Mr. Tom, get that fiddle going," Willie pleaded.

"And you gals," Willie's father cried, "let's see those struttin' shoes a-workin'!"

[45]

A full moon shone down on the merry party. Thousands of stars blinked overhead. But the fires that were kept burning made the Quarters stand out as though it were still daylight.

Tom fiddled till his arms ached and he had to stop. But there were fiddlers in the Quarters who continued their bow scraping. Around Tom whirled the dancers, laughing and shouting.

Tom went off to find Willie. Apparently that boy had a bottomless stomach, for he had stopped dancing and was eating again.

"Tomorrow let's start digging in that Indian mound," Tom said.

Willie stopped halfway through a bite on an ear of corn. He moaned. "Honest, Mr. Tom," he complained, "I thought you had forgotten all about that fool ghost pile. Honest, couldn't you just forget it?"

"Not on your life," Tom answered. "And you're not going to forget it, either!"

"That's the truth," Willie groaned. "All night long I'll be thinking about it!"

CHAPTER FIVE

The Ghost Pile

MORNING sunlight sparkled on the water of the Rivanna. Butterflies fluttered above the tall grass, and the air felt balmy. Tom tied his horse to a tree, then leaned over to scratch Snoop's ear.

"We've got a perfect day to find out what's in that mound," he told his glum-faced companion.

Willie started unpacking the shovels, axes, and scythe. "Why do we care what's in that old ghost pile?" he grumbled. "What good is it going to do?"

"Don't you want to learn what the past has to teach?" Tom asked.

"What does a stableboy need to know about

[*49*]

the past?" Willie demanded. "When I rub down a horse, is he going to care what I got to tell him about some old Indian bones? Just tell me that, Mr. Tom."

"You may not be a stableboy all your life," Tom said.

"Then I'll be doing something else that somebody tells me to do," the other replied.

Tom looked seriously at the scowling Willie. Presently a gentle smile touched the corners of Tom's mouth. "Maybe you won't always be a slave," he said. "Maybe someday you'll be free."

But Willie's scowl only grew longer. "You know the law says I'm a slave forever!"

"A bad law can be changed," Tom said. He twisted his foot against the ground, for what he wanted to say embarrassed him.

"See here, Willie," he blurted, "I don't *order* you to help me dig in this mound. If you'd like to go back to the Quarters, you're *free* to do so as far as I'm concerned."

It was the stableboy's turn to act embarrassed. "Come along," he said awkwardly. "If we're going to upset those old ghosts, let's do it while there's lots of sunshine!"

[*50*]

Tom grinned at the gingerly way Willie crossed the ditch that separated the mound from the low ground of the river. Willie might have been walking on hot coals. And once on the mound, the sweat seemed to ooze out of every pore on Willie's face.

"It's not that warm," Tom joked.

"It is when the spirits are breathing down your neck," the other declared.

"Then why don't I feel them?"

"You will," Willie threatened. "They're just building up to give you a real blast!"

But an hour later Willie's disposition had grown more cheerful. Tom had sunk holes into three parts of the mound and had failed to uncover anything but an occasional rock and a few highly annoyed worms. After a time Willie even chuckled.

"Those old ghosts are well hid," he said happily.

"We'll dig on the side nearest the river," Tom decided stubbornly.

Willie was totally unprepared for the discovery that came half an hour later. Tom's shovel, scraping in the dirt, suddenly stopped. With excitement he pointed at the place where he had been scraping. He had dug only a few inches into the side of the mound.

"Look here," he cried. "There's a whole cluster of bones!"

Willie gulped.

Tom dropped down onto his knees, shoving Snoop's inquisitive head out of the way. Carefully, he scooped out the earth with his hands. Each moment his excitement mounted.

The bones he uncovered were lying in the utmost confusion, seeming to verify Willie's theory that the mound once had been the scene of a battle. The bones pointed to all parts of the compass, and were often entangled with clumps of earth holding them together.

Tom worked feverishly, with Willie's large eyes peering over his shoulder and Snoop trying to sniffle his way into the hole.

"At least keep that hound out of here," Tom grunted impatiently.

It was strange, Tom thought, how bones from the most distant parts of the body were found together. Often a foot bone would be found inside a skull. Why? Because the battle theory was wrong! These bones, more likely,

[52]

had been emptied from a bag or basket, and covered over with earth, without any attention to order.

Willie looked as though he might faint when Tom began passing up bones for him to place on the ground.

"Handle them carefully," Tom warned. "At the slightest touch some of them turn to powder."

"I wish they all would," Willie said.

Yet the collection at his feet grew rapidly. Bones of the arms, thighs, legs, feet and hands took their place in the pile before Willie, who, despite his fears, began to take an interest in what would appear next. But the first skull made him yelp.

"Look here, Mr. Tom, that thing could bite me!" Willie cried.

"Yes, the teeth are still there," Tom said, grinning. "You better watch out!"

Even Snoop shied away from the skull, growling.

As the morning wore on, however, Willie learned there was truth in the saying that familiarity breeds contempt. He grew used to

[53]

handling the bones—even the skulls. A few ribs and the vertebrae of a neck and spine were added to the collection.

Tom came out of the hole carrying a skull smaller than the others.

"Look here, Willie," he exclaimed. "See how smooth the upper edge of this jawbone is? That's the place where the sockets for the teeth should be and they aren't there."

[54]

"They got knocked off," Willie guessed.

"No," Tom said, "they never formed. This is a jawbone of a baby—that's the only thing it can mean. And babies don't fight in battles, so we've blown up that idea for good!"

Willie whistled. "Wait till I tell 'em in the Quarters, Mr. Tom. Some of them think they're so smart, but they'll find out Willie can know a thing or two!"

"Of course you can," Tom cried. "You can learn about anything you like!"

Willie's attitude toward the ghost pile had changed entirely. He became as anxious as Tom to see that the bones were packed carefully in baskets so that they would suffer no damage when they were carried to Shadwell. And Willie grew irritated at the strange way Snoop began to circle the mound and came charging between the boys and their work.

"That dog's acting like he wants to have a conniption fit," Willie growled.

Tom straightened up and watched. He couldn't deny that Snoop acted queerly. The sun now was directly overhead, and blisteringly hot.

"He's going crazy with the heat," Willie predicted.

Tom shook his head. "Listen," he told Willie.

Down the valley came a cry that sounded like "hal-loo, hal-loo!" Then the baying of dogs—of tens of dogs, maybe a hundred of them—could be heard.

In a few moments the dog pack burst into view, with twenty or thirty mounted riders driving hard behind them.

"It's a foxhunt," Willie shouted.

In that instant, below them where the marsh grass was heavy along the bank of the Rivanna, Tom saw a gray flash.

"There's the fox!" he cried.

But the wind already had told Snoop the fox was there. With a spurt, he was down the hillock and across the ditch. Tom had never seen him run so fast.

"I'm going after him," Tom shouted to Willie.

"Come back, Mr. Tom!" Willie demanded. "You're too young for a foxhunt!"

Over his shoulder the other called, "Nonsense! That's my dog! Where he goes I'm going!"

Tom's long legs carried him in swift bounds to the tree where his horse was tied.

"Mr. Tom," Willie pleaded. "You'll get hurt!"

In another instant Tom had loosened the rope and leaped into the saddle.

CHAPTER SIX

Hard Riding

TOM wanted to laugh at the frightened look on Willie's face. The horse, responding to the pressure of Tom's knees, broke into a run. Tom's earliest memory was of the time when, about two years old, he had been placed on a pillow and ridden down the lane at Tuckahoe. Tom couldn't remember ever feeling unsteady on the back of a horse.

The bay mare that Tom rode had a long stride. She liked to lay her ears flat in the wind.

Snoop already had disappeared somewhere ahead with the dog pack. And now the hunters raced along the bank of the Rivanna. A young chap named Carter, who was perhaps sixteen years of age, shouted in contemptuous tones at Tom.

"Get out of here!" Carter roared. "You'll kill yourself."

"I can handle a horse," Tom yelled.

"You'll be thrown at the first fence," Carter bellowed. "Ride out, you fool! Do you want to break your neck?"

Tom's lips tightened. "I'll show you if I can ride," he muttered. Despite Carter's screeching protest, he coaxed the bay mare to a full burst of her powerful legs.

Soon Tom was riding with the leaders to the left of the hounds. He thought that he recognized Snoop, running with head up and stern down. About fifty yards separated dogs and horsemen.

The fields of grass flashed under the pounding legs of the bay mare. The scent of the fox must be very strong, Tom thought, for the dogs made little cry. The chase was veering away from the river toward rolling pasture lands.

Once more Carter appealed to Tom.

"Turn back, you idiot," the youth screamed

[*59*]

over the rushing breeze the horses stirred up. "Here's where the chase really gets tough."

Tom didn't have time to argue. Ahead loomed a fence, the kind that foxhunters call an "oxer." A wide ditch stood behind the fence, which was constructed of solid oak rails set into sturdy posts.

Tom swallowed lumpily, fully aware of the danger that faced him. A short jump and collision with the rails could roll him into the ditch to take his chances under the hoofs of the horses.

"Come on, girl," the boy sang to the bay mare. "Easy does it, girl. Now—*now,* up we go! Get those legs over! Reach that grass beyond the ditch, girl! Hit it gently and don't break stride!"

For a moment all Tom saw was blue, cloudless sky overhead. Then for a long, fearful instant, the treacherous ditch yawned beneath him.

A cry sounded beside Tom. He saw, in a quick glimpse, Carter bouncing ball-like in the ditch, where he had been thrown. The youth, Tom guessed, would be badly shaken —and more injured in pride than body.

The bay mare touched the grass beyond the ditch and sped on. Tom's heart sang. He wasn't going to fail Snoop! Anyone who owned the best foxhound in the Virginia highlands should be able to ride with the best hunters!

Right and left of Tom were half a dozen other riders. They looked at him curiously, but said nothing. Tom soon understood why.

A plowed field, followed by a grass one, with ridge-and-furrow running uphill, made Tom pull at the bay mare. The ridges were "against" or across him—furrows that had been deeply dug and in which a thousand moles seemed to have left their hills.

Foxhunters called this kind of field "sticky," and feared it more than a jump. Tom found himself rolling on his mount and felt like a ship caught in a stormy sea. Three or four riders stopped altogether.

"We're coming, Snoop," Tom gritted through chattering teeth. He clung as closely as he could to the side of the bay mare, a way of riding over trying ground sometimes described as "hugging the wind." Then, with relief, Tom reached grass once more.

Tom's anxious eyes scanned the skyline. The worst obstacle Tom thus far had encountered now confronted him—a strong rail fence *leaning toward him*. The boy scarcely had to look to guess that another wide ditch waited on the other side.

Tom remembered the lessons in riding Peter Jefferson had given him. "There are times, Tom," the man had taught, "that you make a jump or take a tumble by the way you use your hands."

So the boy put the bay mare in a steady hand canter. At the right instant, as the animal leaped, he must drop his hands. He must not miss the proper spot by so much as an inch!

Tom sucked in a deep breath. The bay mare sprang—and *down* went Tom's hands.

Up, *up* climbed rider and horse. At the top of the arc, both seemed to hang for just a second in the air. The ditch sped by and Tom shouted:

"Splendid, old girl! You're the only horse for me!"

A good sportsman on a foxhunt never looks backward, nor did Tom do so now. But he couldn't help noticing that only one other rider was close beside him. He was leading the hunt!

Ahead raced the hounds. When, suddenly, one dog swerved across the field, Tom knew that head straining to a scent. *Snoop!* Tom chuckled.

"Where you go, I'm going," he murmured. That was why he was in this chase, anyhow!

Tom didn't know whether the other rider followed and he didn't care. No quarry was more difficult to catch than the gray fox, for this fellow possessed a color that often blended into the trees and underbrush. The hunt went to the horseman who followed the right dog.

"And there's only one right dog for us," Tom crooned to the bay mare. "When we catch that Snoop, we'll have our fox!"

"The tail is going to be your trophy to keep!"
Mr. Potter said

At the bottom of the next hill stood a group of trees. Snoop barked furiously. Tom, reining hard, found fifteen pounds of frightened fox glowering from its hole in the underbrush.

When in time the other hunters rode up, some could not disguise their disgust that a boy had outridden them. But others thought it was a fine joke, and Mr. Potter, who served as master of the hunt, slapped Tom on the back.

"By George," he cried, "you're as good a young horseman as anyone can find in Virginia! You may have been the uninvited guest on this foxhunt, but you'll be invited on the next. Moreover, the tail that goes to the rider who is nearest to where the hounds catch the fox, is going to be your trophy to keep!"

Tom thanked Mr. Potter. Then, dismounting, he threw his arms around Snoop and hugged the panting hound. Everyone smiled, and someone said, "A real pair of purebreds!"

Tom returned to Shadwell, tired in every bone. Willie already had come back with the baskets from the Indian mound, and also with a story that must have pictured Tom as riding to certain death. Tom felt sorry for the worry his mother had suffered, and yet the fault was really Willie's for spreading a wild tale.

Peter Jefferson could not conceal his deep pleasure in the excellent horsemanship Tom had shown by winning the hunt. The man walked down to the stables with Tom to make certain that the bay mare was rubbed down thoroughly after her hard ride.

"Tom," he said, "I've noticed for a long time that you can do most things better than other boys your age. Before you know it, you'll be a man."

Tom flushed happily.

"Yes, it won't be long before you can be trusted with the full responsibility of a man," Peter Jefferson predicted.

"I shall try to do my best," Tom promised.

Under what sad circumstances, within a very few years, Tom would be called upon to prove the truth of his father's statement was something that neither man nor boy could then foresee. But the present for Tom was surely pleasant. That very night Peter Jefferson wrote to a friend at William and Mary College in Williamsburg. Were the bones Tom had discovered important? They were, the friend replied, and should be preserved with great care. For Tom a lifelong interest in Indian lore had begun.

CHAPTER SEVEN

Tom's Secret

THE canoe was where Tom had left it, tied to the stump of a tree. The boy untied the rope, then, pushing hard with his foot, glided a dozen feet from shore before he started paddling. Sunlight speckled the water of the Rivanna.

From the position of the sun Tom judged that there were still six hours of daylight. Also he was sure that no one had seen him. Even Snoop had been left behind so that Tom could skip away unnoticed. He paddled steadily to reach the opposite bank of the river, and pulled the canoe up into the tall grass.

Tom was fifteen now—a tall, thin, raw-boned boy whose spidery legs carried him across the field in bouncing strides. Once he reached the cover of the woods, his freckled face relaxed. He had made a clean getaway.

Along the trail through the trees Tom walked more slowly. He noticed where a beaver had gnawed the trunk of a tree and

where a porcupine had lost three of its quills. An ache stabbed Tom, for it was his father who had taught him to pick out such marks in the forest. Now Peter Jefferson had been dead almost a year, and another summer was nearly gone.

In a month, Tom would be going back to Parson Maury's school, which meant boarding with old Maury and his family every Monday through Friday. Yet in another year he would be going to college in Williamsburg, and might not get home to Shadwell for months at a time.

Tom scuffed his feet through the leaves. "If they'd just give me the books," he muttered, "I'd teach myself."

And yet he didn't really mean that, either. It had been Peter Jefferson's wish that he finish his schooling at Maury's and go to college.

"Of course I will," Tom told an inquisitive blue jay that looked down at him from a branch. "Only I like it better—well, you know, up there!"

Tom grinned. An occasional blue jay or squirrel or chipmunk were the only ones who ever heard about his secret. Once he had confided in a black snake that he found drowsing by a rock, but that cool fellow had slithered off without the least interest!

The ground now began to rise, but Tom's strides lengthened eagerly. He toiled steadily upward until he reached the summit of the little mountain. Suddenly he could look out for miles—over the valley and the fields of Shadwell and to the distant peaks of the Blue Ridge.

" 'Tis said pirates have their secret hideaways in caves," Tom chuckled. "Well, mine is on a mountaintop!"

Tom wondered what some of the boys at Maury's school might say if they knew how much time he spent here. Likely they thought a mountaintop was one of the loneliest places in the world, which only proved how little they knew!

First, there were the fresh tracks among the trees. Tom examined them closely. They were new or the rain earlier this morning would have washed them away.

"Wolf track," Tom said. Virginia paid a bounty of twenty pounds of tobacco for a wolf pelt. That was a good sum, and for a moment Tom was tempted to fetch the gun that he had hidden in the cache he had built. Two days before, a wolf had killed one of the calves at Shadwell—perhaps this very prowler!

Tom was a true farmer's son. He hated a

wolf. When the beast struck, no calf had a real chance. The urge was still strong to go after the wolf when Tom rolled back the rock that covered his cache. There were the gun and powder horn ready for use. Wouldn't take a moment to set the cap in the firing pan, dump in the powder, and ram down the ball.

"Later, maybe," Tom murmured.

Neither was he interested today in either of the books hidden there. But the wooden mold that held his "experiment" he lifted out carefully. Every secret had a most secret part to it, and the mold held Tom's.

That "experiment" had begun one day when Tom had thought, "I'm happier on this mountain than anywhere else." It was then he decided that someday he would build a house here, but the idea of a brick house came later. The red stickiness of the soil at Shadwell should make good bricks, Tom had reasoned. Shucks, there was nothing to finding out if it would make bricks if you knew what to do. Or if you asked enough questions.

Down in the Quarters, Tom had found a slave who knew how to make bricks. It had been fun. Mixing the reddish soil with sand

and water had given him a thick, mudlike substance to force into the mold. But somehow the sun never dried it quite right. Under Tom's fingers the surface always crumbled.

"It needs to be baked in an oven," he decided. But he was certain just the same that Shadwell could produce its own bricks.

Tom stretched out in the grass with his hands under his head. All summer long he had begun to have ideas about doing different things. One night, writing at a table, he had reached for a book. It had been a nuisance and he had wondered why the top of the table couldn't be made to turn so the book spun around to you.

"Jane said I was the laziest boy in the world," Tom remembered, smiling, "but some day I'll build that table!"

Tom got a lot of ideas from seeming lazy. On rainy days it was a nuisance to go outdoors to see which way the wind was blowing. A weather vane ought to be hooked up somehow so it would give directions indoors. And—

Tom sat up suddenly. Around him the mountain was strangely silent. Tom listened, but no bird sang, no squirrel chattered. Tom knew the kind of telegraphic system among animals that warned them of impending danger. That wolf must have come back!

This time he did not hesitate. Reaching into the cache, his hand found gun, ball, and powder horn.

Up on his feet, the boy strained his ears. Down the mountain a ways there was a spring. Had the wolf come there to drink?

Tom walked cautiously. Again he recalled the calf that had been killed. His temper flared up anew.

His eyes searched every tree as he went downhill toward the spring. His backwoodsman's instincts told him he would be right.

But he wasn't—not at first. When he sighted the spring, it was empty. Tom guessed this wasn't his lucky day. He had missed his bounty for the wolf.

For a moment, he rested against a tree, wondering. The mountain was still tensely quiet. For some reason, cold prickles raised on his neck. He checked the cap in the firing pan—just in case.

Tom's heart beat a little faster, waiting. Nothing happened. But what warning did a calf have when the wolf sprang and its cruel fangs ripped its throat?

Tom watched intently. He could have sworn, to the left of the spring, he had seen the ferns move. Could it have been the wind? Tom brought his musket up against his shoulder. It was a mighty funny wind that blew on one side of the spring and not on the other where he stood.

Taut nerves never made a marksman, Tom told himself. Relax. Feel the gun in your hand. Shucks, this was his secret mountain, wasn't it? Any wolf that thought he could take it over deserved a reckoning!

The ferns moved again. It was still a funny wind, Tom decided. He hadn't felt it.

But then Tom saw the pointed gray ears, the beady, glistening eyes.

He wasn't tense at all. He sighted straight and fired the ball. A crash sounded in the ferns. Tom remained master of his mountain.

There was excitement in the yard at Shadwell when Tom returned, lugging the wolf over his shoulder. In moments the Quarters was almost emptied.

"Mr. Tom got that wolf," the cry went

round. "Ain't no calf-snatcher going to live round here!"

Jane asked, "Where'd you shoot him?"

"Across the river," Tom said vaguely.

"You mean over on the mountain?"

Tom whirled around. His face flushed. "Jane, spying isn't—"

"Isn't nice? No, Tom," Jane said, "it isn't. But couldn't two people love the same place, and take turns loving it, so they don't get in each other's way?"

Tom looked sheepish, but only for a moment. "Well, I'll let you in on the whole secret. Someday I'm

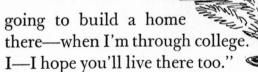

going to build a home there—when I'm through college. I—I hope you'll live there too."

Jane smiled. "I'd like that, Tom," she said. "I'd like that very much!"

CHAPTER EIGHT

Rebellion

TOM knew that he was stared at. Yet now that it was 1762 and he had lived almost two years in Williamsburg, he supposed that most citizens simply took him as an odd fellow and said among themselves, "If Tom Jefferson is queer, it is none of our business."

Still, it was no ordinary sight to see this carrot-topped young man, well over six feet, running along the Duke of Gloucester Street as though a pack of demons pursued him.

Tom's long legs flew up and down with violent strides. His loose arms waved at his sides like rapiers that might cut off any head which came too close. And his mouth, wide open to suck in the air, made him look somewhat like a catfish with a man's body.

*Tom's long legs flew up and down
with violent strides*

Glances of amusement and astonishment followed young Jefferson, as he pounded down the dusty street. Many odors made his long nose twitch—freshly baked bread, polished leather in a bootmaker's shop. A few doors beyond, his nose told him that candles were being poured into molds. He heard the taps of a cabinetmaker's hammer.

On the steps of the wigmaker's shop, a lanky, handsome man, who had watched Tom puffing toward him, called out in a jovial voice:

"Stop a moment, Jefferson!"

Tom pulled up, panting and grinning.

"Up to your old tricks, I see," the jovial man laughed.

"If by 'old tricks,' " Tom answered, "you mean, Mr. Wythe, am I getting my daily exercise, I plead guilty."

George Wythe rubbed his smooth chin that had just been shaved for a penny. "How far do you run every day?"

"About three miles, I guess," Tom said. "There's a stake I've driven in the ground outside of town. Running from the college to the stake and back gives me a chance to really stretch my legs."

Wythe smiled. A pinch of snuff made him sneeze, for even one of Williamsburg's most distinguished lawyers could acquire a bad habit. George Wythe had been watching Tom's progress. He knew the boy was quick-witted and brilliant. Now the man asked curiously, "How many hours a day do you study, Tom?"

"Usually fifteen or sixteen, sir."

" 'Tis no wonder you stand at the top of the heap at William and Mary College," Wythe declared. "But you'll soon finish your course there, and then what?"

A bit self-consciously, Tom ruffled his red hair. He would not have left his wig in his room had he anticipated this interview. He said, "I had thought of reading for the law— under you!"

"Then that you shall," Wythe answered heartily. "It will be my honor, lad!" The rumble of a coach, drawn by six horses and filled with ladies in feathers and fine silks, cut off his voice for a moment. He added, "I hope you haven't forgotten your engagement at the Governor's Palace this evening. Be sure to bring your violin."

"I shall," Tom promised.

A second pinch of snuff set Mr. Wythe off on another bout of sneezing. "Well, get along on your spin, Tom," he managed at last. "I'll see you later."

Tom's long strides soon were whisking him along the Duke of Gloucester Street. The stares resumed and followed him all the way back to his room at the college. But what care he? Queer he might seem to some, but not to those who really knew him.

Sometimes Tom felt guilty over how Williamsburg made him forget Shadwell. He liked the college—even the hard seats that kept the sleepiest student awake. He liked

most his freedom. His love for horses often led him to the race track.

As the provincial capital of Virginia, Williamsburg teemed with people. Planters came to attend the Assembly or the sessions of the court, and Raleigh Tavern or Chowning's Tavern never had room for all. But men who

[83]

wanted to argue all night scarcely needed beds.

"The King, sirs, will bankrupt us with his taxes," Tom heard them shout.

Tom heard of duels that grew out of these arguments. When he went to reading law under George Wythe, dueling was one of the first subjects he'd explore. It was a practice that he felt should be outlawed.

George Wythe, sneezing over his snuff, welcomed Tom into his law office when at last the youth finished his studies at William and Mary College.

"I won't have to worry over you," Wythe chuckled, "unless you study *too* much. Some day you'll be my finest student."

"I shall try, sir," Tom said.

"Try tomorrow to remember to bring that violin," Wythe added, "and we'll find time to scratch out a tune or two."

Tom nodded and grinned.

If anyone had asked Dabney Carr, who was Tom's best friend, what sort of fellow Jefferson was, Dab would have told him:

"A marvel! He needs no more sleep than a bird and excels at everything he undertakes!"

Dab had known Tom since their schooldays at Parson Maury's. Through two years at college they had shared a room. To Tom, Dab was like a comfortable old shoe—most pleasant to have around. Moreover, he suspected that his younger sister Martha and Dab intended to marry one day.

A year after Tom had begun reading law, he and Dab still lived together.

Another young lawyer, so poor that he couldn't afford lodging at the tavern, often shared the room that they occupied. Taking Patrick Henry in off the streets was chiefly Tom's idea, however. Dab had serious doubts about Patrick.

"He's a firebrand," Dab warned. "He may die on the gallows some day!"

"Not Patrick!" Tom laughed. "With his gift for making speeches, he could even talk his way out of that!"

On the stairs sounded the step of the very person they had been discussing. Patrick never opened a door. Rather, he flung it before him, as though he enjoyed seeing it wobble on its hinges. Nor did Patrick really ever sit in a chair. Instead, he bounced into a seat, as though it were an animal waiting to attack him that he must overpower by surprise.

Tom laughed every time Patrick sat down with a thud.

"I tell you, there's got to be a stop to him!" Patrick shouted.

"To whom?" Tom asked.

Patrick looked disgusted. "To the King, of course!"

Dabney sighed. "You're off again!"

Patrick snorted. "I am poor enough right now," he growled, "without that knave in England taxing me to death without my consent!"

"You'll be accused of listening to the idlers in the taverns," Tom said.

"Bah!" Patrick scoffed. "By whom? The idlers themselves? The times change and not for the better. In 1765 George the Third is even worse than he was in 1764!"

Tom had to agree. The King couldn't seem

to understand that the American colonists felt as freeborn as any Englishmen. And why did the King think he had to place garrisons of soldiers to keep watch over the colonists, and then make the colonists themselves pay the Stamp Tax to provide the money for those garrisons?

"No one should tax us but ourselves!" roared Patrick. "Has the King forgotten it was Caesar's tyranny that drove Brutus to kill him? Has he forgotten it was the tyranny of Charles the First that caused Cromwell to behead him? That fathead of a King shall hear me speak out against his Stamp Act!" Patrick thundered.

"Where will you speak?" Tom asked.

"In the halls of the Virginia Assembly," Patrick snapped, "where a free man has the right to be heard!"

Patrick jumped up and paced the floor. Then, as suddenly as he had entered, he stomped out of the room. Again the door bounced on its hinges.

Tom looked seriously at Dabney. "Patrick's anger is not without sound cause," he said.

[*87*]

"Are you another the King may have to send to the gallows for his ideas?" Dab asked.

"Would you stand by and let me hang?"

"No, by George, not while there was a breath left in me," Dab exclaimed.

"Then let us hope the King listens to men like Patrick," Tom said. "If ever Virginian is forced to defend Virginian, who can guess what the end might be?"

Dab did not try to answer that question.

Apparently Patrick told everyone he met of his intended speech. The streets of Williamsburg throbbed with a rising excitement. Next morning Tom was caught up with the crowd that headed for the State House. Even the entrance to that building teemed with people. Determinedly, Tom pushed his way to the door of the hall where the debate over the King's Stamp Act was already in progress.

Tom felt a sudden chill. Patrick's magical voice had been raised. First he argued that people in the colonies had all the rights of people in England. Therefore they must decide what taxes were to be imposed. To de-

Patrick's magical voice had been raised

stroy freedom in America, Patrick warned, was to destroy it also in England.

Now he shouted:

"Caesar had his Brutus, Charles the First his Cromwell, and George the Third—"

People looked shocked. Then, from every part of the room, the cry rang out: "Treason! *Treason!*"

Patrick stood with his proud head lifted.

"I tell you," he roared, "that George the Third may profit by their example. If this be treason, make the most of it!"

Tom shoved his way back into the sunlight. Outside the State House the world seemed as calm and peaceful as ever. Yet the echoes of Patrick's voice pounded in Tom's head. He would never forget this speech.

CHAPTER NINE

Tom Loses a Fight

TWICE that year of 1765 Tom came home to Shadwell. His first visit was gay, for Dabney Carr and Martha Jefferson were married. Then in October Tom again made the long journey into the highlands, his heart heavy with grief. His beloved sister Jane had died.

One evening Tom slipped out of the house and hurried down to the Rivanna. He found the canoe in its old hiding place. Grimly, he paddled across the stream and climbed the path to his mountaintop.

Sad and lonely, Tom closed his eyes as if to see a dream. Again he promised himself that he would build a house and someday raise a family. Perhaps in time he would have daughters of his own, with black hair and saucy eyes, to remind him of Jane. Meanwhile he would return to Williamsburg and work harder than ever at his law books.

For the next five years Williamsburg knew Tom as a rising young lawyer who had learned almost every law Virginia ever had passed. Dabney Carr and even George Wythe nodded good-humoredly when Tom wanted to change many of the laws. If he really thought dueling should be outlawed, they teased him, let him prepare a bill to submit to the Legislature. And if he thought it outrageous that a woman who talked too much could be ducked in the public pond, let him draw up another bill preventing that.

But one day in 1770 Tom reached a decision that shocked even easy-going Williamsburg. That day a young mulatto boy walked into Tom's office. The lad possessed a long face and a high nose, much like Tom himself. His chin rose in a stubborn tilt.

"I'm Sam Howell," the boy said.

Tom broke into a smile. "Don't tell me you need a lawyer, Sam!"

"I sure do," Sam Howell said, so deadly earnest that both eyes blinked. "I need a law-yer awful bad."

Tom stroked his chin and tried to hide the smile that was almost a grin. "You in trouble, Sam?"

"I want to go to court," the boy answered.

"Oh," Tom said, "you want to get someone else in trouble! Who, may I ask?"

"Yes, sir, Mr. Jeff'son," Sam rushed on. "I'll tell you. It's my old master—that Mr. Nether-land, the planter. I want to take him into court and sue him."

"Sue him," Tom repeated. "For what?"

Sam Howell drew a deep breath. "I reckon he didn't have any right to buy me for a slave," he said. "I reckon I can sue him for my free-dom!"

Common sense told Tom to send the boy on his way. Young slaves weren't supposed to sue their masters. Instead, Tom said, "Tell me your story, Sam."

Both of Sam's eyes were blinking again. "Well, sir, Mr. Jeff'son," he began, "my grandmother was a slave, and the law says that

[*93*]

her child, who was my mother, had to be a slave. But the law don't say that the grandchild, who is me, has to be a slave!"

Tom thought for a moment. The boy was right! In 1723, a law had made slaves of the children of parents who were slaves, but that law had never been extended to include children of later generations.

"Yet you were sold into slavery?" Tom asked.

"To Mr. Netherland," Sam said. "Only it wasn't fair. My grandmammy, she remembers the law. You look it up, Mr. Jeff'son. You'll see."

Tom nodded. He took a book from a shelf and began to thumb through the pages. Really, Tom was stalling for time to think. There was only one chance in a thousand, or perhaps in ten thousand, that a case like this could be won. If the court upheld Sam Howell, it would almost end slavery in Virginia!

Then Tom glanced across at Sam. The boy stood, proud and defiant, and Tom thought with a chuckle, "He's got the spunk of six mules!" Tom said aloud, "All I can do is *try* to win for you, Sam."

"You give it a good try, Mr. Jeff'son. I don't ask more." Suddenly the lad's confidence wavered. "Now about paying you, Mr. Jeff'son, I—"

"There won't be any fee," Tom said gently.

Later, he stood by the window of his office and watched Sam going down the street.

"Six mules," Tom muttered once more. Inside, he began to feel uneasy. Among his friends, he never doubted, he would be stirring up a hornet's nest. But Tom's eyes followed the figure of the boy. He wanted to win for him. He wanted to win Sam's case more than any case he had ever taken.

In time, on the calendar of the Virginia court Sam's case was listed. *Howell vs. Netherland,* the words read, but what they meant was *Slave against Master,* and many faces scowled, reading those words.

Tom also scowled, but for another reason. Mr. Netherland not only intended to fight Sam but had secured the best lawyer he could to help him—George Wythe!

Dabney Carr, arriving in Williamsburg on a visit a few days later, found Tom working furiously on Sam's case. Law books littered Tom's desk, but most of the time Tom paced the floor, hands clutched behind his back.

"Dab," Tom cried, "I'm going to say things nobody will like. I don't care. Sam Howell deserves to be free, and they'll just have to listen to me!"

Dabney sighed sadly. "But you own slaves yourself," he said. "They run Shadwell for you and make you one of the richest men in Virginia. If you should win for young Sam—and I don't think you can—you'd be hurting no one more than yourself."

"That isn't important," Tom answered. "For seven years, when we all lived at Tuckahoe, my father gave up his own home to keep a promise he had made. Defending Sam Howell, when I believe he is right, is also a matter of putting honor first."

Dabney repeated a rumor he had heard. "Is it true that you're going into the Virginia Assembly and fight for a law whereby a master, if he chooses, can free his own slaves?"

Tom guessed that Dab wanted to tell him he would lose this battle also. "I expect to lose," he said.

The other threw up his hands. "You're beyond my understanding, Tom." But admiration rather than reproach filled Dabney's voice.

The day of Sam's trial came too quickly for Tom, who read and thought, read and thought, searching for the words that would help the boy. Dab sat in the courtroom that morning. Tom, in wig and gown, looked strangely tense and belligerent beside the jovial Wythe. Mr. Wythe boasted his client was so clearly favored by the court that once Tom had been heard, the case would be thrown out without further argument.

Tom groaned. He hated to think how near to the truth Wythe could be! A sick emptiness seized him.

Quietly, Sam Howell waited. The boy's face had been scrubbed until it shone and he was dressed in a neat homespun jacket and breeches.

Tom looked away. The unhappy inward

[*97*]

feeling mounted. Sam deserved a better lawyer than he. Tom even worried over the
scratchiness of his voice. He disliked talking
in court, for he always sounded shrill and rasp-
ing.

But when that morning Tom began to talk,
seeing Sam in his mind though his back was
turned to the boy, Tom's earnestness softened
the harshness of his tones. It was true, Tom ad-

mitted, that the law of Virginia had extended slavery from parents to the boys and girls born to them. But wasn't there a law that stood above Virginia law—the law of nature?

The judge gave a start. Tom plunged on.

"Under this law," Tom cried, "all men are free!"

Tom didn't care if the judge stared at him. God was the Author of this law of nature.

"Would you defy Him?" he exclaimed. "You have done so once by enslaving the parent, and you have done so again by enslaving the children of that parent. But you must make a new law, if you can find a legislature *wicked enough* to do so, before you can enslave the grandchild!"

When Tom finished, the room was still. Wythe coughed. The judge looked pale and shocked. Then anger tinged his cheeks. "The case is dismissed," he said icily.

Sam Howell's head lifted proudly. His eyes met Tom's.

"Mr. Jeff'son," he said, "it was fine to hear."

Tom patted Sam's arm. He felt choked, and, turning quickly, left the courtroom. Outside sunlight flooded the streets of Williamsburg.

Dabney Carr came out to join him.

"Well, Dab," Tom muttered, "you were right. It all got me nowhere."

But Dabney said, " 'All men are equal.' That's what you said, Tom. A chill ran down my spine when I heard you."

"I shall go on saying it," Tom promised. "I shall say it over and over till I'm listened to."

The sun brought out the reddish glints in the young man's hair. The head of Thomas Jefferson also lifted proudly.

CHAPTER TEN

A Day of Prayer

A BITTER wind howled through the high-lands of Virginia. Snow fell heavily, and in places the drifts were three and four feet deep. Along the road through the forest, that fearful January night in 1772, two riders on horse-back struggled through the wind and snow.

"It isn't more than a mile farther," Tom shouted to the pretty young woman who rode on the other horse. "You must think me an awful fool to bring you out into this!"

"But I'm as anxious as you to reach my new home," the young woman shouted back. A few days ago her name had been Martha Skelton. Now she was Mrs. Thomas Jefferson.

Tired and chilled to the bone, the couple at last reached Tom's mountain. The snug brick house that Tom had built was dark and silent, for Tom and his bride had not been expected on such a terrible night and all the servants had gone to bed.

"We won't wake them," Tom said. "We'll build our own fires and get our own supper and show the whole world what a happy, self-reliant couple we are!"

Tom's wife laughed. "Tom, Tom," she teased, "I do believe the Lord gave you big feet because He knew how much you would want to stand on them as the most independent man in Virginia!"

Tom grinned and began building a fire. The cottage consisted of a parlor, kitchen, hall, bedchamber, and study, and in each of the rooms Mrs. Jefferson lighted candles so that her new home soon glowed cheerily. Then she began preparing their midnight dinner.

"Some day," Tom declared, "when we have built the main house, Monticello will be the finest place in Virginia!"

"I love that name," the new Martha Jefferson said. "Isn't it an Italian word?"

"It means 'little mountain,'" Tom said. "Everyone around here thought I was crazy when I had the top of this mountain scooped away for this home, but I'm used to being considered an odd fellow. And when I insisted on making my own brick, they thought me crazier

[*103*]

still, for the belief in the highlands is that wood is better than brick for shedding the rain."

The fire now was roaring, and the house had grown warm and comfortable. "We picked the right night to prove how wrong they were," Tom's wife exclaimed gaily. "After we eat, Tom, fetch your violin and we'll play duets until dawn, because this shall be a merry home!"

In another hour, Mrs. Jefferson was seated at the harpsichord, and Tom stood at her side, fiddle under his chin. Outside the snow still fell, the wind still howled. Music and laughter within the house on Tom's mountaintop rang out, challenging the weather.

Yet troubled times were ahead. Tom often had to leave Monticello to attend the sessions of the Virginia Legislature, to which he had been elected. The long journey to Williamsburg was not easy. Often four or five miles of wilderness separated the plantations that he passed. But Tom always carried a small violin on which he fiddled away to amuse himself during these lonely stretches.

In time, however, even the violin was put
aside, for what Tom heard in Williamsburg
filled his heart with anger and sometimes with

fear. After a while, each new journey to the
provincial capital seemed to lengthen the lines
of worry around Tom's hazel-gray eyes.

[*105*]

Tom's frown was never more pronounced than during 1774 when a beautiful spring crept into the highlands of Virginia. Martin, the house servant who felt Tom was his personal charge, grew as fidgety and concerned as his master.

"You don't get out in the air enough," Martin scolded Tom. "All the time sitting in here thinking and writing will just make you sick."

Tom smiled faintly. His glance fell on the pages scattered across the table. At the top of one of the pages he had written in bold letters: *A Summary View of the Rights of British America.* Tom told Martin, "If I can't make the King see what harm he is doing, we may all be quite sick!"

Martin snorted. "These king troubles," he growled. "I hope you give that old George what-for so he'll listen!"

"I think I'm giving him what-for," Tom chuckled. "But King George is either a very stubborn or a very stupid man, Martin. He isn't going to like being told that the law of nature gives men the right to make their own laws. Or that while we owe loyalty to the King, continued unjust acts by the King can forfeit that loyalty."

Old Martin nodded. "You just tell him. That's what he needs, all right. A good hard talking to!"

Well, Tom thought, the pamphlet he was writing would supply at least that. "I'm expecting Mr. Nichols," he informed Martin. "Will you bring him in here the moment he arrives?"

Old Martin's eyes widened. If a big man in Virginia like Robert Carter Nichols was coming to Monticello, then the "king troubles" must be boiling for sure! "Yes, sir," Martin promised. "I'll bring Mr. Nichols right in!"

It was toward midafternoon that the servant reappeared with Tom's expected visitor. Nichols was a grave, dignified man who greeted Tom with a solemn bow. The door to the study was closed.

"Let me show you the new writing table I had built," Tom said. "See, you just sit in this chair and spin the top to get what you want."

"It's a lazy man's dream," Nichols exclaimed.

[*107*]

Tom grinned. "And yet you don't really call me lazy, do you?" he asked, motioning to the many pages of writing that covered the table top.

Robert Carter Nichols found a chair by the window and stretched his legs. "No," he admitted. "I don't. Still, I can't hold with all of your ideas, Jefferson. I heard you speak in the Assembly last month. You said that a few selfish Englishmen planted slavery among us when we were young colonies and had to accept anything. You can't blame the King for everything!"

Tom answered seriously, "I know I have severe critics—even enemies, if you like—as a result of those views. That is why, Nichols, I appeal to *you* now to make this new stand against the King."

The two men fell into an earnest discussion of the new crisis that faced the colonies as a result of the foolish Tea Act of 1773. Because they were charged a tax on tea brought from England, the colonists preferred to drink Dutch tea on which there was no tax. The King wished to stop them from buying the

Dutch tea. In December, he had passed a law making the price of English tea lower than that of Dutch tea, even though the tax still had to be paid. This the colonists still refused to do, and now they were in revolt. In Boston the tea had been dumped into the harbor.

"And what does the King do?" Tom flared. "Boston is to be punished. Its port is to be closed to all trading ships, and troops placed in its streets. Why? Because the people in Boston refuse to pay that tax, they are to be stripped of their personal liberty!"

"Boston is a long way from Virginia," Nichols muttered.

"That is the very point," Tom cried. "The King believes that we cannot stand together and therefore thinks we can be abused separately."

Nichols drummed his fingers on the arm of the chair. "When is the port of Boston to be closed?" he asked.

"June first."

"So you want me to ask the Virginia Assembly to make that day one of prayer to show our sympathy for this great injustice to Boston?"

"The King must know," Tom declared, "that the hostile invasion of Boston is resented everywhere in British America. We must stand united for a common right!"

Robert Carter Nichols stood up. "If the King doesn't heed our warning, what then?"

"The people in Boston are being enslaved," Tom answered. "We may be next."

Nichols breathed deeply. "All right," he said. "I'll introduce the resolution. Virginia shall stand by Massachusetts, and when on June first you pray, ask that the King may be made to understand."

Tom arose. His deep-set eyes looked solemn. "It is God who gave us life and God who gave us liberty," he replied. "The King's argument is with God—not with us!"

CHAPTER ELEVEN

The Man in the Clouds

TOM'S worries over what Martin called his "king troubles," lessened for a time. One reason for this was the publication of Tom's pamphlet by the Virginia Assembly. There had been a few who had argued against publication, and had felt the pamphlet would do more harm than good, for in *A Summary View of British America* Tom had renewed his attack upon the "infamous practice" of slavery.

Yet with Tom's belief that "the God who gave us life gave us liberty at the same time" almost everyone in the colonies agreed. When Tom warned that "the hand of force" could destroy this union of life and liberty, most heads nodded. *A Summary View* was read in

[*111*]

all thirteen of the colonies, and everywhere men began to say, "Down in Virginia there's a chap named Tom Jefferson who has a real head on his shoulders!"

The name of Thomas Jefferson was suddenly famous even in England, for here also his pamphlet was read. Britons began to argue that maybe Jefferson was right. Americans should decide their own taxes. It was wrong to station troops in America.

"Our problems may yet be solved by men of good will," Tom thought happily. But there was still another reason why the very walls of Monticello seemed to burst with merriment.

Almost a year had passed since the visit from Robert Carter Nichols when one day the door to Tom's study was flung open. A little girl, with eyes as saucy as anyone could wish, bounced into the hall, screaming happily. Close behind her came a pair of long legs.

"Wait till I catch you," Tom shouted at his young daughter. "I'll teach you to climb up on my chair and keep me from working!"

Laughing boisterously, the child scampered away. The two-and-a-half-year-old youngster

fled like a rabbit, but Tom caught her at the
end of the hall. He lifted the little girl, kicking and wriggling, over his head.

"One, two, who are you?" Tom sang.

"Martha!" screamed the child. "Martha
Randolph Jeff'son!"

"Who's your mommy?" Tom demanded, swinging the child in a wide circle.

"Martha Skelton Jeff'son," the little girl shrieked.

Chuckling, Tom hugged his daughter, then carried her to the door. Outside they could see the vast dome of the sky. Soft clouds drifted overhead. For just such days as this, Tom had invented a special game.

"Is there a man in the clouds?" he asked.

"Giddap! Giddap!" cried little Martha.

"Oh," said Tom, feigning surprise, for a game without surprises is poor fun, "he's a man on a horse?"

"Clop, clop, clop, clop," the child answered, imitating a horse as her father had taught her to do.

"Is he a big man?" Tom questioned.

"Big man," Martha said. "Two miles high —like you!"

Tom grinned. "What is the man doing?"

"Got gun," Martha declared.

"Is he hunting a bear?"

"Bang, bang," screamed Tom's daughter.

"Did he shoot the bear?"

[*114*]

"No, no!" Martha Randolph Jeff'son wriggled furiously in her father's arms. "He shoot old King!"

Tom set down his daughter. This wasn't the ending he had taught her!

"Why, you little rebel!" he exclaimed. "You've been hearing too much grown-up talk!"

Martha Randolph Jeff'son had a mind of her own. She ran back along the hall, shouting, "Bang, bang! Old King dead!"

Tom shook his head.

In succeeding weeks Tom kept shaking his head—but for another reason. Hours of heated debate in the British Parliament had produced a strange document known as "Lord North's Proposals." All right, this document said, the colonies could decide their own taxes, *but*—

And that *but* kicked the legs out from under the whole offer, for the *amount* of taxes to be raised would be decided in England!

Once more the pen of Thomas Jefferson scratched over long sheets of foolscap, and his *Reply to Lord North* came to be no less famous than *A Summary View*. Once more he tried to warn the British that they were asking free Americans to choose between "death or submission."

Tom's hope that there could be a peaceful remedy to the "king troubles" had died before the spring of 1775 when he prepared to make the long journey to Philadelphia. Leaders from all the colonies had joined in a group called the Continental Congress. This group was really the first step toward an independent American nation. George III continued to demand absolute obedience to his unfair laws, and the Continental Congress was formed as though the colonists had said, "United we stand and divided we fall."

Tom paced his study. He hated to leave Monticello. He could see that his wife was pale and ill.

But it was she who insisted that he go. "It is your duty, Tom," she said, speaking a word he could never resist.

On June 11, Tom reached Williamsburg, which always had seemed a long journey in itself, but nine days more of coach travel still faced him.

Sometimes he drew forth his little fiddle and amused himself for a while. But usually he was too tired to care. A bed along the way might consist of no more than a sheet and a bag of feathers for a mattress. Meals were poor and slowly served. And the coach seat, though padded, was uncomfortable, bouncing over deeply rutted roads!

At Baltimore a man of high, jovial spirit joined Tom in an inn where he stopped to rest. He was a talkative fellow, who said:

"The ride from here to Wilmington, Delaware, will be bad enough, so let us stop scowling at one another."

Tom asked, "Where are you from, sir?"

"Boston," the other replied. "Where they dumped the tea into the harbor, in case you've forgotten." The man laughed. "My name is Adonijah Maxim, and I'll fight the man who says George the Third has a brain left in his head."

Tom smiled. His new companion had the air of a seasoned traveler. Good food or bad, good beds or bad no longer could upset his easy-going disposition. After a time Tom inquired:

[*117*]

"How stands Massachusetts today?"

"Ready to fight—if we have not already fought," the Bostonian answered. "We Yankees will defend our liberty with guns—or pitchforks—as we get the chance."

"George the Third feels his soldiers will be more than a match for you," Tom commented.

"Does he now?" Adonijah Maxim chuckled. "We have men who carry their guns with them day and night—to work, to meals, to bed. We call them Minutemen because they are ready at any minute to fight the nosy British. Now, sir, may I ask your name?"

"Thomas Jefferson. From Virginia."

"Ah, yes," Adonijah said. "You wrote that pamphlet. You are famous. You are against slavery."

"Very much against it," Tom declared.

Adonijah Maxim leaned back in his chair and closed his eyes. He seemed not to have heard Tom. Then he said, "Perhaps you are right, Mr. Jefferson. Time will tell."

CHAPTER TWELVE

"I Shall Be with Them"

AT LAST Tom's coach rattled over the streets of Philadelphia. Tom liked this big port city with its busy docks, its brick and stone houses, and its wide, regular streets. But he was a farmer's son, and the rolling fields of Monticello came first in his heart.

Philadelphia throbbed with excitement. British troops, ordered to put down the rebellious farmers of Massachusetts who were determined to keep their freedom at any cost, had clashed with the Minutemen at Lexington and Concord. Then at a place outside Boston that some said was Breed's Hill and others declared had been near-by Bunker Hill, a bloody battle had been fought between the British and the "Continentals," as the American soldiers were called.

Everybody knew that war had come. Nothing else was discussed in the taverns. And on the day before Tom reached Philadelphia, Congress had acted to give the "Continentals" a general who could lead them to victory. Tom knew well this great Virginian, George Washington, who had been named Commander in Chief of the Continental Army. Washington had proved his great qualities as a military man in leading the Virginia Militia in the French and Indian War. Now, overnight, Washington had become the city's idol.

"He'll lick those Redcoats!" Philadelphians shouted.

"You've never seen such a strapping fellow," others insisted. "He's every inch as solid as an oak."

Tom felt sick inside. These were brave words—and largely empty words. Washington's army at best would be a rag-tag group that he would have to whip into fighting trim. There could be no easy war between America and Britain. Now that George III had taken the fateful step to enforce "absolute submission" he would spare no chance to win—even to hiring foreign soldiers, if necessary.

And yet, under these circumstances, the very calmness of Washington was inspiring. Tom wondered if ever he had admired a man more. "He is tall, proud, free," Tom thought. "He is a man to make Virginia feel honored that he is her son."

On the next day Congress planned to see Washington off in grand style on his journey to Boston. There would be bands and a troop of light horse cavalry. All of the delegates from Massachusetts intended to accompany Washington to the outskirts of Philadelphia. But other delegates were equally anxious to pay this tribute to the commander. Tom promised himself, "I shall be with them."

Tom mingled with the other delegates. A grave, dignified man whose eyes, peering over his glasses, could not conceal a twinkle, stepped forth to intercept him.

"Mr. Jefferson?" the man asked.

Tom nodded. He did not need to be told

[*121*]

who was the man addressing him. In the colonies, even Washington was not more distinguished. "It is a pleasure to greet you, Mr. Franklin," Tom said.

"I have read your writings with great pleasure and profit," Benjamin Franklin continued. "We shall have great use for your pen here."

"I hope that will be of service," Tom declared. "I am not much as an orator, I am afraid."

"Nor am I!" Franklin's twinkle deepened. "We poor fellows will have to do the best we can. Is it not so, Mr. Jefferson?"

Tom smiled. With pen and sword, Virginians were being asked to lead the fight for American freedom. At once Tom felt warm toward Benjamin Franklin. "I have found a real friend," he thought, making one of the best guesses in his whole life.

On the morrow, Tom stood with the delegates from Congress who were seeing Washington off. The drums rolled, the trumpets blared. Work in Philadelphia stopped as people jammed streets, windows, doorways to catch a glimpse of the great man. Then an enormous shout went up, for Washington had appeared, sitting tall and straight on his horse.

For an instant Tom closed his eyes, remembering what little Martha had seen in the clouds that day—a big man with a gun on a horse who was going to "shoot the old King!"

"How near the truth my little rebel came," Tom muttered affectionately.

CHAPTER THIRTEEN

Voice of Independence

THE war dragged on for a year without any real result. Washington held Boston under siege, and for months his army seemed motionless. An American force invaded Canada, attempting to make that country the fourteenth colony, but this effort ended in failure.

At least one third of the American colonists remained loyal to George III, among them Governor Dunmore of Virginia. The Governor boarded a British warship that attacked coastal settlements and finally burned Norfolk. If these outrages were not enough to make Southern tempers flare anew, a small British force sailed southward, hoping to rally sympathizers in the back country of South

Carolina and take the vital port of Charleston. But the Southern fighting spirit was aroused, and this British plan was smashed in the battle of Moore's Creek Bridge near Wilmington, North Carolina.

Tom felt the strain. Twice he had been home to Monticello, and had been re-elected to Congress. But his wife's health was no better, and a second daughter named Jane had died when only a year and a half old. In the spring of 1776, he returned to Philadelphia a sad and worried man.

Yet the purposes of the Continental Congress had grown bolder, and Tom faced his duties squarely. One day a Virginian, Richard Henry Lee, rose in Congress and said it was time the colonies declared to the whole world that they were now an independent, united nation, and would never stop fighting until they were free of England.

Tom heard himself named to the committee that was to write this Declaration for Congress. Crusty John Adams, the Massachusetts firebrand, was another committee member. And with deep pleasure Tom found that Benjamin Franklin also was one of the group. Connecticut was represented by a shrewd Yankee named Richard Sherman, and powerful New York sent a brilliant man named Richard Livingston.

Tom, one of the youngest men in Congress, thought that the first drafting of a document so important would fall to the great John Adams, but here he met with a surprise.

"No, no," Adams told Tom. "You ought to do it."

"Me?" answered Tom. "Why?"

John Adams barked out his sentences: "Reasons enough. Reason first—you are a Virginian, and as a member from our most populous colony you ought to appear at the head of this business. Reason second," continued Adams, who knew perfectly well what others thought of his sharp tongue, "I am obnoxious, suspected, and unpopular. Reason third—you can write ten times better than I can."

Tom sighed. Mules chained together couldn't budge Adams from an idea once he had fixed his mind to it. "Very well," Tom said. "If you have decided, I will do as well as I can."

Later that day Tom walked through the streets of Philadelphia. His one thought was of the enormous responsibility that had been placed on his shoulders. Coaches rattled by, a boy chased a dog almost between Tom's long legs, and from a tavern a song drifted out:

"Yankee Doodle keep it up,
Yankee Doodle dandy . . ."

But Tom neither noticed nor heard these distractions. The weather had turned hot and sticky and hundreds of green-winged horse-flies droned through the air. Tom brushed away the pests with an absent-minded impatience. Perhaps, Tom told himself, he may have shocked the court when, in pleading for the freedom of Sam Howell, he had argued that under the law of nature all men are equal. Yet when a country declared its independence and renounced its master, wasn't it doing so for the same reason?

Tom reached the brick house on the southwest corner of Seventh and Market Streets, where he had rented the second floor for his own quarters. Here he sat at a folding desk, scratching with his pen to express this one thought that seemed so important to him. In time he felt that he had said what was in his mind and heart. He read over his words, hoping they were all right and never guessing that what he had written would become the rallying cry of all people who wished to be free:

"We hold these truths to be self-evident: that all men are created equal; that they are endowed by their Creator with inherent and inalienable rights; that among these are life, liberty, and the pursuit of happiness; that to secure these rights, governments are instituted among men, deriving their just powers from the consent of the governed . . ."

The important word was "inalienable." It meant that men had rights of freedom no one could take from them, for these were God-given rights above the authority of kings or judges or other government officials.

Day after day Tom toiled at drafting the Declaration Congress wanted. He accused George III of trying to enforce "an absolute tyranny" over the colonies. Tom was a trained lawyer who knew that the case against the

King must be argued from facts. Point by point, Tom wrote down the evidence of this tyranny.

The King, Tom declared, had refused to consent to laws necessary for the public good. He had not allowed the colonists to have any voice in their own government. He had not held proper elections. He had made judges in the courts dependent on him for their salaries, so that justice had become a matter of doing what the King wanted.

"He has plundered our seas, ravished our coasts, burnt our towns, and destroyed the lives of our people," Tom wrote in another passage. Bitterly, Tom accused the King of bringing armies to subdue Americans, of capturing fellow citizens on the high seas and making them go to war against their friends and brothers, of encouraging Indian savages to attack the settlers. George III, Tom wrote, was "a tyrant" who was "unfit to be a ruler."

Still Tom was not satisfied. There was one thing more he must say, even though he knew he would become thoroughly unpopular for saying it. Yet if all men were created equal, slavery was cruel and evil. Tom thought for hours about this problem. He wrote angry words about a King "determined to keep open a market where MEN should be bought and sold." He had seen them die on the ships that had carried them into captivity. This, Tom declared, was "war against human nature."

The hot days of June went by. Congress was impatient to receive the Declaration. One day John Adams visited Tom and read the document he had prepared. Adams slapped his leg with delight at the long paragraph attacking slavery.

"But your Southern friends will never let that stand," Adams said.

"I fear my Northern friends as well," Tom answered. "They own the ships that make the profit carrying slaves across the seas."

Adams looked down his nose. "I don't like calling the King a tyrant," he said. "That sounds too much like scolding."

"King George is a tyrant," Tom replied stubbornly.

"Let Franklin make up his mind about that point," Adams said, not wanting to have an argument with Tom. Adams understood the hard days that were ahead for Jefferson. The Declaration of Independence would be debated word by word until all the delegates in Congress were satisfied with it.

Gravely Benjamin Franklin read the draft. He had only a few small changes to suggest. Then Franklin peered over his glasses at Tom.

"You know what's ahead?" Franklin asked.

"They will tear it apart, I suppose," Tom muttered. "I am not a debater. I can only sit and listen and wish it were over."

Franklin's smile was kindly. "You have done well," he said. "You must be patient with others who may not think as you do."

Tom's draft was reported to Congress, and soon the debate began. Tom sat through three miserable days as tempers sometimes became as hot and sticky as the weather.

One group of revisions changed only words or dropped phrases and sentences to shorten and make the meaning clearer. In his fine opening Tom had written that men were endowed with "inherent and inalienable rights," but the delegates thought this should read

[*131*]

'You have done well, Mr. Jefferson!'

"certain unalienable rights," which was a small change, indeed.

Franklin told Tom, "A large group of the delegates feels that we have friends still in England and that there should be no statements that give offense to the people of England."

Tom nodded a bit grimly. But the attack on his passage about slavery was harder to bear, for every word was struck out! South Carolina and Georgia especially were insistent that nothing on this point should be included, since their interest in a continuing importation of slaves was strong.

Tom paced the floor of Congress. Adams stopped him once.

"It is as I told you," he said.

"The North does little to help," Tom flung back.

Adams placed his hand on Tom's shoulder. "See how much is left. This is your document —almost entirely your thought and very largely your language. You have done well, Mr. Jefferson—perhaps better than I had hoped."

Tom slapped at a horsefly. Next to the

building where Congress met stood a stable. With the mugginess of early July the stable had seemed to produce thousands of new green-winged pests to annoy the delegates.

"I swear," Tom told Adams, "this debate might go on forever if we could stand the flies!"

Adams chuckled.

At last, on Thursday, the fourth of July, 1776, a motion to adopt the Declaration of Independence was passed. With the end of the debate, the tension was swept away. The mood of the delegates grew jovial, and many stopped Tom to congratulate him on the great work he had performed.

"Well, we have done it," John Hancock said. "We have declared ourselves free and must now hang together."

"Yes," commented Benjamin Franklin with a twinkle in his eyes, "we must hang together or we shall all hang separately."

And stout, heavy Benjamin Harrison turned to a fellow delegate, Elbridge Gerry, who was a very small man. "When it comes to hanging," Harrison teased Gerry, "I shall have the advantage, for you will be kicking in the air when it is all over with me."

Tom broke into a smile for the first time in three days. Men who could declare themselves

In Philadelphia's main square a crowd gathered

free could dare to joke over the hangman's noose.

On Monday in Philadelphia's main square a crowd gathered. The Declaration was to be read by Captain John Hopkins, the young commander of the first armed brig of the navy of the new nation. Captain Hopkins mounted the platform and faced the multitude. His booming voice carried across the square as he pronounced that "all men are created equal," and that governments must rest on the consent of the governed.

Tom could feel the crowd responding to these words. Men nodded their heads as Hopkins stated each reason why this action had been taken and we were now a free and independent country. Even in that part where Tom called George III a tyrant unfit to rule there were nods and cheers.

Later, excited Philadelphians entered the State House and ripped down the King's coat of arms. A fire was built and this symbol of the King's power thrown onto the blaze. Thunderous cheers rose from the crowd.

Many of the delegates had to return to their

own colonies and report on what Congress had done before they could sign the Declaration. So it was not until August that the formal sign-

ing could occur. First to write his name with bold strokes of the pen was John Hancock.

"There," Hancock said, "John Bull can read my name without his spectacles!"

CHAPTER FOURTEEN

Escape from the Redcoats

TOM came home to Monticello. He would have been glad to quit public life and give his whole time to his books, his plantation, and caring for his wife. But Martha Skelton Jefferson simply smiled when Tom paced the floor and spoke of never again leaving Monticello.

"Tom," she said sensibly, "your Declaration of Independence can mean little unless each state passes the laws that make people free. Here in Virginia you must lead that fight."

Tom sighed. He knew that his wife was right. So, during the next five years, he saw even less of Monticello. He was tremendously proud of the victory he won for religious freedom. It took years to achieve that triumph. But Tom, convinced he was right, thrust forward that stubborn chin.

Only the Church of England, later called the Episcopal Church, was approved by Virginia law. A Quaker or Methodist or a member of any other sect had no right to preach his religious beliefs. Tom couldn't see this restriction as true religion. He said so, and kept saying so, until the law was changed.

Virginians liked Tom. The first elected Governor of Virginia was Tom's old friend, Patrick Henry. In 1779 this high office went to Tom himself, and the following year he was re-elected Governor.

Then the year was 1781. Tom had returned to Monticello under circumstances that he did not like in the least. Twice, to escape British troops, the capital of Virginia had been moved —from Williamsburg to Richmond, and again from Richmond to Charlottesville. But the Redcoat army was still loose in Virginia.

"You know what those British want," grumbled old Martin, who had grown bald in service to the Jeffersons. "Those British want to capture *you*."

"You're joshing me," Tom laughed. "The Redcoats wouldn't go to all that trouble for just one Governor."

Old Martin said, "Humph! You're not just a Governor. You're the man who wrote the Declaration of Independence. They'd like to get you, all right."

"You think they'd hang me, Martin?"

"Not you," Martin declared. "They'd ship you off to England and let the people pay to get a good look at such a famous troublemaker."

Underneath Tom felt uneasy. "Perhaps you had better make sure the carriage is ready, just in case we have to move the family," he told Martin.

The old man nodded. "Your own horse is at the blacksmith's," he said. "Shall I fetch him back?"

"No, the horse needs new shoes. Anyhow," Tom added, "I don't think we'll see the Redcoats away back here. It's just that Mrs. Jefferson isn't feeling well, and it will comfort her to know she'll be cared for no matter what happens."

"Yes, sir," Martin answered. "I understand."

But what he really understood was the fact that Tom was worried. Not many minutes later Tom's long legs could be seen hurrying along the road to a rise that commanded a good view of Charlottesville. Under his arm he carried a spyglass.

When Tom came to the rise, he stood for some minutes searching the countryside across the valley. It was just as he had thought—the British were nowhere in sight.

"Maybe Martin will be satisfied now," he murmured, feeling much better.

He started the walk back, but after a short distance realized that he had lost his sword-cane. More than likely it had dropped out of its sheath up there on the rise. Tom retraced his steps, and, as he expected, the sword-cane was in the road.

"As long as I'm here, I might as well have another look," he thought. Again he squinted through the spyglass.

Tom gave a start. Everywhere around Charlottesville were flashes of red uniforms!

Tom kept his head. Even a British cavalry detachment wouldn't find its way across the valley to Monticello in less than three or four hours. He would send his family to a neighboring plantation, where they would be safe until he could join them. And then, even though he ran the risk of capture, there were many official papers that he must destroy before the Redcoats reached Monticello.

Old Martin needed no more than one glance at Tom's sober face to guess the truth.

"I'll fetch the carriage," he said.

[*143*]

Tom's wife took the news bravely. "Join me when you can, dear," she said.

Nine-year-old Martha cried, "Daddy, if any Redcoat comes near me I'll make an awful face and stomp on his foot!"

Tom hugged his older daughter. "You just behave like a lady," he warned. Then he leaned over and kissed young Polly, who still seemed little more than a baby.

Tom waved good-by when the carriage drove off. A frown creased his brow as he walked back to the house. When his second term as Governor ended he would leave public life and give his wife all of his care.

Of course he would be severely criticized. Whenever Washington had asked for troops, Governor Jefferson had sent Virginians to fight in New York, New Jersey, and Pennsylvania. Now, with British invaders as far inland as Charlottesville, those who cried that Tom had left his own state unprotected would raise an even angrier shout.

"They'll say that's why I'm resigning," Tom thought bitterly. "They'll say I'm running away!"

Tom paused. Looking across the fields of Monticello, he remembered the day when his father had made him help harvest the tobacco rather than dig in the Indian mound. He had learned that day to put duty first. Now he owed a duty to his wife.

"I must do what I think is right and let others think what they will," he said aloud.

Old Martin had become a bundle of restless energy. A boy had been sent to the blacksmith's shop for Tom's horse. Another boy had been posted on the road to watch for the Red-

[145]

*Tom burned those papers that must not
fall into British hands*

coats. A third, named Caesar, ripped up a plank on the porch.

"That's where we're going to hide the silver," Martin explained. "They're not going to get that to help make fat old George the Third any richer!"

Tom had to smile. Quietly, for the next two hours, Tom sorted his papers and burned those that must not fall into British hands.

The boy Martin had posted on the road came running hard.

"They're almost here," he cried. "Old Master had better get."

Tom came out onto the porch. Martin was still carrying silver that he passed down to Caesar, who was under the porch.

"I'll go across the fields and along the banks of the Rivanna," Tom said. "They won't find me. You're in charge, Martin, but don't take any foolish chances."

"Run along," old Martin said crossly, and Tom's smile lengthened at the thought of how often the servant managed the master. But he was on his horse in a few brisk strides and rode at a gallop when at last he dropped from sight over a hill.

Nor had Tom escaped a moment too soon, for the British cavalry detachment burst into the yard at Monticello. Martin was so flustered that he slammed the plank onto the porch, forgetting that poor Caesar was still down there (and it wasn't until three days later that Martin remembered to release that badly frightened, half-starved youth).

A British captain strode up to Martin. The Redcoat drew his pistol.

"Where's Mr. Jefferson?" the officer demanded.

"I don't know nothin'," Martin grumbled.

"You'll tell me or I'll fire," the Britisher cried.

Martin looked steadily at the pistol. "Fire away then," he said. "Maybe when I'm dead you can get me to talk."

The officer hesitated, then lowered the pistol. "You Americans don't know when you're beaten," he growled.

"Because maybe we're not beaten," Martin growled back. He turned and sauntered into the house. In a way, it was understandable that he forgot about poor Caesar imprisoned under the porch!

Meanwhile Tom rode easily along the Rivanna. The man who as a boy had won a foxhunt over this same country had no fear of being caught by the Redcoats. Even if Martin could be made to tell which way Tom had gone, the British would not catch him.

"Martin won't talk," Tom guessed correctly. "And he'll kill anybody else who might!"

Within a few days the British left Charlottesville, and Tom and his family returned to Monticello. Then his term as Governor

"Where's Mr. Jefferson?" the officer demanded

ended and he refused re-election. The criticism was as severe as he had expected, but Tom didn't care. He was with his wife, who needed him. Tom could never stand to be idle, so now, in spare moments, he began writing a book called *Notes on Virginia*. Into its pages went such things as the Indian mound and Ontasseté's story of the big buffalo. The book, when published, made Tom more famous than ever.

That year Martha Skelton Jefferson died. Tom could not conceal his grief. Suddenly he could not bear Monticello with all the memories of his wife whom he loved so dearly.

"I will go back into public life," he thought. "Just for a little while."

The country surely needed Tom, for with Washington's victory over the British at Yorktown the long war ended. The new nation had to bind up its wounds and shape its government.

Tom served two years in the federal Congress. His inventive mind devised a new system of coinage, dividing American money into dollars and cents.

[*151*]

When debates arose over what to do with the great Northwest Territory, Tom was back in stride, fighting for one of his oldest beliefs. Tom took a map of this great region, placed his finger at Lake Erie, drew a line southward, and argued that after the year 1800 slavery must not be permitted in any territory west of that line. In time most of Tom's idea was adopted. And the principle that a part of America existed where slavery never would be allowed had been written into one of the laws of the land.

By then Tom was in France, helping Benjamin Franklin and John Adams draw up commercial treaties with European nations. In 1785 he succeeded Franklin as minister to France.

So Tom's "little while" in public service grew longer and longer. After a time it seemed as though there might never be another end to it.

CHAPTER FIFTEEN

The People Grow Mad!

JEFFERSON is a rascal!"

"Jefferson is a danger to the country!"

"Fiddlesticks! Jefferson is a great hero!"

In the early weeks of 1801 everyone in America had an opinion either *for* or *against* Thomas Jefferson.

A strange crisis faced the country. Each state, according to its population, had a certain number of delegates who voted for the President and Vice President of the nation. These delegates formed a group known as the Electoral College. Whoever received the highest number of their votes became President, and whoever had the second highest number was Vice President.

No one really ever had expected the Electoral College to produce a tie vote.

"What does it mean?" the people asked, reading the result. "There it is, as plain as day, 73 votes for Thomas Jefferson and 73 votes for Colonel Aaron Burr!"

"It can mean only one thing," others replied. "The election now must go to the House of Representatives, and nine states must agree on a candidate before we can have a new President!"

"When will they vote?"

"February 11th."

"What happens if nine states can't agree on a candidate?"

"They'll have to keep voting until they do!"

Excitement mounted as pages were ripped from calendars to show that the month of February had arrived. In the nation's new capital in Washington men walked along Pennsylvania Avenue, so intense in their arguments that they forgot the swamps on both sides of this thoroughfare were famous for producing chills and fever in anyone lingering near them.

The heated words went on day and night:

"The people want Jefferson!"

"Then the people are crazy!"

"There will be riots if Jefferson isn't elected!"

"Riots, eh? I told you he was a trouble-maker!"

Sometimes the only calm man in Washington seemed to be Thomas Jefferson. Each morning at Conrad's boarding house he took his usual seat for breakfast at the end of the table. He talked pleasantly, but he appeared more interested in the reported discovery of some ancient bones than in the debates of which he was the central figure. Yet Tom wasn't spoofing his audience. He *was* more interested in the old bones.

Tom's very calmness infuriated his opponents. They cried, "Judge him by the facts. He did more than anyone to wreck the Constitution and try to hinder us from becoming a real country!"

"That isn't true," snapped those who supported Tom. "He only asked why the Constitution, as first written, did not protect such rights as free speech, a free press, freedom of religion, and trial by jury. As much as anyone he fought for the first ten amendments to the

Constitution that protect these personal liberties!"

Many wealthy persons especially despised Tom. "That filthy Democrat," one of them sneered. "If he stepped into my house I'd throw him out!"

"Because he won't lick your boots like Alexander Hamilton?" Tom's supporters flung back. "Hamilton wants to rule the state governments and the people in the states. He'd be King Alexander the First if he could! Well, Tom Jefferson had the spunk to fight him. He insists that the people must be left free to govern themselves, even to raising taxes!"

One thing was certain about the shouting that filled the air. The angrier the charges and countercharges grew, the more unfair they became.

Tom said nothing. He had fought Hamilton's belief that the few should control the many, and he couldn't deny it. Yet he had served his country in every way he had been asked—as minister to France, as Secretary of State under President Washington, as Vice President under President John Adams.

Tom's friends made much of these last four years in office. As Vice President, Tom had presided over the Senate of the United States. Was there anyone who could say he ever had been unfair?

"There was your real Thomas Jefferson," those friends shouted. "A man devoted to honor! Even though he hated the policies of Hamilton and his gang, he always insisted that they be treated squarely in the Senate!"

Tom waited for February 11th and the fateful voting in the House of Representatives. He disliked Aaron Burr much more than Hamilton. Burr was clever, but Burr tried to appeal to both political factions and Tom wanted to beat him. A man should stand for fixed principles!

Washington's residents awoke on the day of the voting to a raging snowstorm. Drifts piled high in the streets, and no carriages moved. But the blizzard couldn't break the tension. Up the hill to the Capitol building Congressmen struggled on foot, determined that their votes should be counted. Poor Nicholson from Maryland, who was ill, insisted that he be car-

*Up the hill to the Capitol Congressmen
struggled on foot*

ried to his place on a stretcher. His wife came with him, staying at his side through the long hours that followed, and giving him medicines between ballots.

"I'm for Jefferson," Nicholson cried. "Maryland is so closely divided, it could go for that scoundrel Burr if I missed my vote!"

Outside the chambers of the House of Representatives the people awaited the results. Despite the storm, messengers waited to relay the news to taverns and boarding houses.

Toward late afternoon the seventh vote was completed. The messengers raced off with the result.

"How stands it now?" everyone asked.

"The same!" came the excited reply. "Eight states for Jefferson. He still needs one more!"

"What states are divided?"

"Maryland and Vermont."

"Will they keep on voting?"

"Through the night, if necessary!"

The snow stopped. The long night wore on. Mr. Nicholson rested on his couch, drank his medicines, and had the ballot box carried to him so that he could drop in his vote. Then it was morning, nineteen separate votings had been taken, and the result was unchanged.

Tired and cross, the Congressmen kept balloting at intervals of an hour. On the twenty-seventh voting Jefferson still held eight states, and Maryland and Vermont were still divided.

"Recess! Recess!" the legislators cried. "We need time to rest and think."

So the balloting was halted until the next day.

But there was one person who could not rest. Alexander Hamilton had fought Tom Jefferson with all his might, but Hamilton knew that Tom was honest where Burr was at least unreliable and might even be unscrupulous. Hamilton made a decision that placed his country first, as he saw it. How many letters he wrote in support of Tom no one ever knew. From morning to night he sat at his desk, urging his friends by letter to vote for Tom.

On February 13 there were only two ballotings and the House of Representatives recessed again. The following day the Congressmen tried three times more without success to break the deadlock.

An unruly spirit began to sweep Washington. Mobs roamed the streets in an ugly mood. The possibility of public riots was now far from an empty threat!

"Hurrah for Jefferson!" went the shout. "We want Jefferson for President!"

"Down with Burr!" sang another crowd. "Give us honest Tom Jefferson!"

Secretly the delegates from Vermont met.

The letters from Alexander Hamilton were read.

The seventeenth of February was a Tuesday. Still the excitement mounted in Washington. The delegates struggled up the hill to the Capitol, and an air of strain filled the room where the House of Representatives met. Another voting began—the thirty-sixth.

But among the Congressmen from Vermont there was an excited commotion. This sudden flurry of raised voices could only mean one thing—Vermont was going to break its tie. On this ballot it would go either for Jefferson or Burr!

Eyes sped rapidly toward the Maryland delegation. Yes, here, too, a change was coming. Here, too, voices were pitched higher.

"It's going to be Jefferson," the rumor started.

"Vermont's for Jefferson! Maryland's for Jefferson!"

The rumors were true. At long last the verdict had come. "A new President! Thomas Jefferson's the new President!"

The news raced through the streets of

Washington. Hats were thrown into the air, songs burst forth, toasts were raised to celebrate Jefferson's election.

Next morning at Conrad's boarding house Tom Jefferson came down for his breakfast looking as calm as ever. The other boarders stood up.

"Mr. President," one said, "you should sit at the head of the table."

Tom smiled. "I feel no different today from what I did yesterday," he answered. "I'll sit in my old place, if you please."

Tom would know how truly popular he was with the people when on March 4th he was inaugurated to the highest office that his country could give. The snows had gone, the streets had thawed, and Washington had become a sea of mud.

Still the people came in crowds to cheer Tom. The roar of artillery saluted the new President. From Maine to Georgia, the cry ran, work had halted and the country was giving itself a national holiday to show anew its respect and affection for the author of its Declaration of Independence.

[*163*]

At ten o'clock that morning a military troop came to escort Tom to the Capitol. Soberly he took the oath of office. He was not, as he had once told Benjamin Franklin, much of an or-

ator. And yet what Thomas Jefferson said that day in his inaugural address people remembered.

Jefferson promised that he would do every-

thing in his power for "the happiness and freedom of all." With typical humility he told his listeners: "I shall often go wrong through defect of judgment." But he would do his best—his honest best. And he said something more —a shining passage that would be repeated across the land time and time again. "Error of opinion may be tolerated where reason is left free to combat it," proclaimed Jefferson, who believed above everything else that a man who loved God must also love liberty.

The people, listening, looked up at a plainly dressed man. He seemed to be one of them, and they were happy.

CHAPTER SIXTEEN

Old Carpet Slippers

FROM his first student days in Williamsburg Tom Jefferson had grown used to being pointed out as a person who went his own way without caring what others thought. Now that he had become President of the United States he was as strong-minded as ever.

One of Jefferson's closest friends during these first years in the White House was a young man who had grown up in the highlands of Virginia not far from Charlottesville. This bright, vigorous youth was Meriwether Lewis, and Tom had called him to Washington to be his personal secretary.

Often the President and his young friend laughed heartily over how shocked some people in Washington were by Tom's behavior.

"Mr. Merry, the British ambassador, declares that you have insulted his country," Meriwether Lewis remarked one day.

"Because he called at the White House in a splendid uniform, wearing a sword, and I re-

[*168*]

ceived him in a pair of old carpet slippers?"
Tom asked.

Lewis nodded.

"Do you think he'll want to declare war on
us as a result?" Tom chuckled.

"He already has declared war on *you,* from
all I can hear," the other said.

Tom shrugged. He knew that he wasn't the
dignified President Washington and John
Adams had been. Both of his predecessors had
acted with grave formality. They always had
been dressed in a courtly manner, bowed at
the right moment, and held dinners where
they were careful to see that the most important visitor had the seat of honor.

Tom would have none of this bother. When
he held a dinner, people could sit anywhere
they liked, for he wasn't going to worry over
who felt he or she was more important than
someone else. As long as his clothes were clean
and neat he didn't see what harm was done if
they were also comfortable. And he liked his
old carpet slippers. Somehow, wriggling his
toes, he seemed able to think more to the
point.

[*169*]

"The people believe in you," Meriwether Lewis said with admiration.

"And I believe in a government that serves the people," Tom answered.

The kind of laws for which Tom fought made him immensely popular. Under John Adams, who had grown into an easily ruffled old man, the Sedition Act had been passed and anyone who wrote or said anything that Adams considered contrary to official policy—that is, contrary to what he believed—could be sent to jail. Thomas Jefferson could never tolerate such a law that destroyed freedom of speech and press. Among his first acts as President was to let out of prison all who had been arrested and convicted under this dangerous law.

So the people knew that Tom Jefferson was no aloof, mysterious dictator who lived in the White House. When he said internal taxation should be abolished, he meant it. Selecting a young wizard in money matters named Albert Gallatin to be his Secretary of the Treasury, he did abolish such taxes while finding other means for paying the costs of running the government. Likewise the law by which the foreign-born must wait fourteen years to become citizens of America seemed too severe to Tom, and again he fought for a fairer law.

"We are a young country," Meriwether Lewis heard him say. "We have yet to grow, especially in the West where there is still a land we hardly know."

For a moment Tom closed his eyes and seemed lost in a dream. He was remembering the boyhood tale Ontasseté had told him of the big buffalo that had leaped over the Ohio, the Wabash, the Illinois, and the Great Lakes. Was the big buffalo still living there, as Ontasseté had declared?

Suddenly events happened in Europe that were to make Tom remember this dream many times. Spain had secured from France the Louisiana territory with its great port of New Orleans. To American settlers in the West, there was only one way they could trade with the outside world and that was down the Mississippi River to New Orleans. In 1803, Spain decided to close the port to such shipments.

Tom's old carpet slippers were heard on the floor of the White House during many long, sleepless hours. The great dream of the country's growth in the West was being strangled! Then, to make the matter worse, Spain gave the territory back to France. Napoleon Bonaparte, the ruler of France, was a warlike fellow, and nobody knew for certain just how far he might go in his ambition for conquest.

One thing was certain—Tom didn't want Napoleon controlling the great Mississippi Valley. Tom talked to Gallatin, and studied his maps to see what harm Napoleon could do by some hostile act if he took the fancy to do so. Then Tom sent a Virginian, James Monroe, to Paris to see if Napoleon wouldn't sell the island where New Orleans stood.

Napoleon fooled Tom completely. France was preparing for a war with England and needed money. France claimed territory in America from the Rio Grande to Canada—more territory by almost one and a half times than the land the young nation then controlled. How would Jefferson like to buy it all? Napoleon would sell it cheap—America could have it all for a mere fifteen million dollars. "It is a noble bargain," Napoleon said.

As the saying goes, Tom had jumped from the frying pan into the fire. Napoleon wanted a decision at once. But did Tom have the right to make this purchase? Might he not have to ask for an amendment to the Constitution before he could make this sweeping decision?

Tom fought with himself. Bargain or no bargain, was it right to do this? Yet if he hesitated too long, and Napoleon changed his mind, might not he be doing his country a disservice by failing to make this Louisiana Purchase? The risk was great, if his political enemies wanted to say, "Look at Jefferson—he tries to fool you in those old carpet slippers but even Alexander Hamilton couldn't be more high-handed than he."

Tom made up his mind. He'd run the risk, for the country's future hung in the balance. He'd sign the papers, buying all of the territory France claimed, and hope that Congress would approve the action.

In the Senate the vote to support Tom was 26 to 5, and in the House of Representatives

[*173*]

the purchase was approved 90 to 25, so Tom needn't have worried.

"I wonder just what I have bought," Tom said one day.

The eyes of Meriwether Lewis began to shine. "There is one way to find out, sir," he cried.

Tom nodded. "We can send out an expedi-

tion," he agreed. Then, looking down at his eager young secretary, he asked, "Would you like to go?"

"More than anything in the world," Meriwether Lewis told the President.

William Clark, who had been a lieutenant when Lewis had served in the army, was selected to help lead the expedition that made both men famous as explorers.

For Tom, following on his maps the route taken by these brave Americans, the vastness of the great territory he had bought became clear. What a wonderful thing he had done! Starting from St. Louis, Lewis and Clark traveled 8,000 miles, reaching the Pacific Ocean in Oregon.

Often, during the years that Lewis and Clark were away, strange gifts came to the White House for the President. Once there were grizzly bears that Tom kept in the White House garden.

"There's Jefferson's bear garden," people in Washington joked. There were other wonders sent back by Lewis and Clark that Tom showed his visitors.

"Here are a pair of stuffed antelopes from the Rocky Mountains," he told his callers. "And that's the skeleton of a prairie wolf. These are Indian clothes worn by the Sioux, and look at these furs if you'd like to see some beautiful ones." Then, from animals taken along the Bighorn, Tom exhibited furs of the red fox, white hare, marten, and yellow bear.

But other of the President's interests that Meriwether Lewis understood brought still more gifts—a box of plants, a box of insects, and cases containing a burrowing squirrel, a prairie hen, and four magpies, all alive!

That Tom had great sport when such ship-

Tom kept grizzly bears in the White House garden

ments reached the White House, everyone knew. It was like those boyhood days being up on his secret mountain and knowing the wolf was there when the ferns moved, because the wind wouldn't blow on one side of the spring and not on the other.

Tom never forgot that mountain. When his second term as President ended, Jefferson easily could have been elected again. No, Tom said. One man should not be President too long. He knew the people loved him, trusted him, wanted him. But he trusted them, and they could always find another leader.

So Tom at last went home to live at Monticello. Always there were people coming to see him—those who had known him and others who simply respected his name and his achievements and wanted to look on his face and say to their grandchildren, "I met Tom Jefferson once."

All were received graciously. And Tom's mountain home astonished them. There was a weather vane in the porch ceiling that told the direction of the wind. There was a clock that could be seen indoors and out. There were windows that opened in pairs, so that you pulled one and the other swung back automatically.

The flowers were beautiful. Tom's plants came from all over the world, and he watched them with affection and knew to the inch how tall they grew. Across the valley in Charlottesville was a beautiful new university that the master of Monticello had designed. He would sit in a window, spyglass to his eye, and watch the buildings going up. That was more fun, really, than looking for hostile Redcoats.

Sometimes visitors to Charlottesville witnessed a rare sight, for there, talking together, might be seen three former Presidents of the United States—Jefferson, Madison, and Monroe.

Thomas Jefferson lived to be eighty-three. He died in 1826, on the day he made immortal in American history—the glorious Fourth of July.

About the Author

Earl Schenck Miers was born in Brooklyn, New York. He went to public schools in New York and New Jersey, and graduated from Rutgers University. For seven years he was editor of the University Publications of Rutgers, and later became director of Rutgers University Press. Ever since then, he has been active in the publishing field, both as a writer and an editor. However, the increasing popularity of his delightful stories for youngsters, as well as his adult books, is forcing him to give more and more time to writing.

About the Artist

Reynold Pollak was born in Vienna, Austria, where he went to the Academy of Fine Art. There he won the Masterschool Prize for Graphic Art and, later, the Golden Fuger Medal. He had traveled widely in Italy, Yugoslavia, France, Switzerland, Cuba, and Canada, but finally made his home in the United States. His work has appeared in leading magazines and newspapers, and his extensive study of eighteenth century culture makes him particularly fitted to illustrate THE STORY OF THOMAS JEFFERSON. And, like Jefferson himself, Mr. Pollak's hobby is building a house.

Signature Books

"Names That Made History"

ENID LaMONTE MEADOWCROFT, *Supervising Editor*

1 Born at Shadwell, Albemarle County, Va., April 13, 1743

2 Becomes the master of Shadwell when his father dies, 1757

3 Enters William and Mary College, Williamsburg, Va., 1760

4 Marries Martha Skelton, January 1, 1772

10 Dies at Monticello, Va., July 4, 1826

9 Arranges for the purchase of Louisiana from France, 1803